TIME

FIRSTS

TIME

Women Who Are Changing The World

FIRSTS

INTERVIEWS · PHOTOGRAPHS · BREAKTHROUGHS

PORTRAITS BY LUISA DÖRR

TIME

Editor-In-Chief: Nancy Gibbs
Creative Director: D.W. Pine
Director of Photography: Kira Pollack

Editors: Claire Howorth,
Siobhan O'Connor
Designer: Christine Dunleavy
Photo Editors: Tara Johnson,
Natalie Matutschovsky
Photographer: Luisa Dörr
Producers: Spencer Bakalar, Diane Tsai
Associate Editor: Abigail Abrams
Reporters: Sarah Begley, Eliza Berman,
Samantha Cooney, Eliana Dockterman,
Lucy Feldman, Ashley Hoffman,
Alice Park, Lily Rothman, Julie Shapiro,
Alexandra Sifferlin, Sade Strehlke
Contributors: Charlotte Alter,
Tessa Berenson, Melissa Chan,
Merrill Fabry, Mahita Gajanan,
Barbara Maddux, Katie Reilly,
Maya Rhodan, Julia Zorthian
Copy Editors: Anny Kim,
Jennifer Schiavone,
Courtney Harris Weingarten

Time Inc. Books
Publisher: Margot Schupf
Editorial Directors: Anja Schmidt,
Kostya Kennedy
Production Manager: Hillary Leary
Prepress Manager: Alex Voznesenskiy
Editorial Production: David Sloan

© 2017 Time Inc. Books

Published by Liberty Street,
an imprint of Time Inc. Books
225 Liberty Street
New York, New York 10281

LIBERTY STREET and Time Books
are trademarks of Time Inc.

ISBN: 978-1-68330-068-7
Library of Congress Control Number: 2017941458

First edition, 2017

1 QGT 17

10 9 8 7 6 5 4 3 2 1

To order Time Inc. Books Collector's Editions,
please call (800) 327-6388, Monday through Friday,
7 a.m.-9 p.m., Central Time.

We welcome your comments and
suggestions about Time Inc. Books.

Time Inc. Books
Attention: Book Editors
P.O. Box 62310
Tampa, Florida 33662-2310

timeincbooks.com

Time Inc. Books products may be purchased for business
or promotional use. For information on bulk purchases,
please contact Christi Crowley in the Special Sales
Department at (845) 895-9858.

Credits

About the photographer

Luisa Dörr is based in Itacaré, Bahia, Brazil. Her photography focuses on portraiture using the iPhone. Dörr's photographs have been published by TIME, CNN, the *New Yorker, Wired,* VICE and other outlets, and her work has appeared in exhibitions in Brazil, the U.S., Spain, France, Portugal, England and Russia. In 2015, Dörr was selected for the LensCulture Emerging Talent and as a PDN (Photo District News) Emerging Photographer.

About the project

TIME interviewed these 45 women in person and by phone over the course of many months. Dörr's photographs, extended interviews with the subjects and a series of thematic films can be found at **time.com/firsts.**

Contents

Giant leaps for womankind

By Nancy Gibbs

S *he broke the glass ceiling.* What a jagged image we use for women who achieve greatly, defining accomplishment in terms of the barrier rather than the triumph. Talk to women about the forces that drive them, and they hit notes of joy and fascination—a passion for music or molecules or fastballs or food that took them places their sisters and mothers had not gone before. "Sometimes even now when I'm told I was a 'first,' it comes as a surprise," says Patricia Bath, a pioneering physician and inventor. "I wasn't seeking to be first. I was just doing my thing."

We wondered if there is some common motive or muscle shared by women who are pioneers. The women profiled here range in age from 16 to 87 and have flourished in public service and private enterprise, explorations to the bottom of the sea and to the outer orbit of Earth. They have been on journeys to places they could only imagine and frequently encountered people who said they would never get there. The stories of success are knitted with stories of setbacks, and these women often credit the people who tried to stop them as a motivating force.

"I recall visiting the home of friends, and a man who was present asked me what I wanted to do one day," says molecular biologist and Nobel laureate Elizabeth Blackburn. "I said, 'I'm going to be a scientist.' And he said, 'What's a nice girl like you doing going into science?' I was shocked and so mad that I didn't know what to say in response. So I kept my mouth shut, but I was all the more determined. In a way, I'm quite grateful to that man."

The first woman to reach a pinnacle may not want anyone to notice her gender; there she is up where the air is thin, where men still outnumber women, but she made it on her own wings; gender is irrelevant, it's the altitude that is awesome. But why are there so few women up there with her? Why did it take this long? And if the answer is even partly that there were few role models, there were no ladies' rooms in the halls of power, if every step was steeper, harder, then women need to stand up, stand out, be seen at every level, for every talent and discipline. "If the person who gets to tell the story is always one kind of person, if the dominant images that we see throughout our lifetimes have been dominated by one kind of person, we internalize it, we drink it in as fact," observes filmmaker Ava DuVernay, who describes Hollywood as a white man's world: "That is a deficit to us. A deficit to the culture."

At the same time, many of these women extol the men in their lives—an older brother as a first competitor, a father who set no limits. "If your dad believes in you, that's important to young girls," says philanthropist Melinda Gates. "If your dad thinks you can be good at math and science, good at business, good at anything, it lifts your confidence and your self-esteem." Former Attorney General Loretta Lynch recalls how her father, a Baptist minister, defied convention and invited women to preach at his pulpit. "The aspirations and dreams he had for my brothers were the same ones he had for me," she says.

Famously successful figures often develop a thick skin in the face of criticism— as when a flock of supercilious French chefs came to Alice Waters' renowned restaurant and declared, "That's not cooking, that's shopping." Or as TV star Issa Rae put it, "There's so much subtlety in the sexism and racism in this industry that you either have to call it out and risk being shunned, or move past it and find your own entryway. I'm definitely in the latter category."

But a thick skin can disrupt sensitivity; what's remarkable about many of these women is their ability to remain empathic, accessible in the face of resistance and ridicule. Many women discussed their moments of failure, of rebuke and how the criticism was often a fuel. "Raising hackles means you're not being ignored," says former poet laureate Rita Dove. "You're pushing the conversation forward."

Our goal with this book and the extraordinary project on TIME.com is for every woman and girl to find someone who moves them, to find someone whose presence in the highest reaches of success says to them that it is safe to climb, come on up, the view is spectacular. They were candid about their challenges, aware of their responsibilities, eager to tell the stories that will surprise and inspire. We hope everyone, at every life stage, will encounter an insight here that will open a door to new ambitions. As former Secretary of State Madeleine Albright always says, "There is a special place in hell for women who do not help each other." But the reverse is also true and more uplifting; there is a special place in heaven for women who shine the light and share it with others.

In 2013 Gibbs became the first woman named editor-in-chief of TIME magazine.

"THEY HAVE BEEN ON JOURNEYS THEY COULD ONLY IMAGINE."

Madeleine Albright

First woman to become U.S. Secretary of State

"There is plenty of room in the world for mediocre men, but there is no room for mediocre women."

Before I became Secretary of State, when I was teaching at Georgetown University, I always told my female students to be prepared to speak and to interrupt when necessary. When I walked into my first meeting of the United Nations Security Council, there were 15 seats and 14 men—all looking at me.

I thought, Well, I don't think I'll talk today. I don't know who everybody is … I want to figure out if they like me, and I want to kind of get a feeling for things. Even though I had advised all of my female students to speak, I myself hesitated. You are worried that whatever you say could sound stupid. Then some man says it and everybody thinks it's brilliant, and you think, Why did I not talk? Which is why I used to advise my students all the time to be ready to interrupt.

That day, I looked down at the table and saw a plaque that read THE UNITED STATES OF AMERICA. And I thought, If I do not speak today, the voice of the United States will not be heard. When I finally did speak, it was the first time that I represented the country of my naturalization, the place where I belonged.

An experience I think all women have, and I have often, is of being the only woman in the room. But if we are in a meeting, we are there for a reason—not to just sit there and absorb but to state what we believe in. We can and should contribute. If you do not, then you should not be in the meeting. If you are there but you are not speaking, you may create the impression that you are not prepared to be there or that you have no business being there. Then you are made to feel inferior, because you are just a fly on the wall.

If you are going to speak, you need to know what you are talking about and you need to do it with a firm voice. And if someone disagrees with you or you disagree with them, try to understand where they are coming from—*compromise* is not a bad word. But I do think that women have to earn respect. It is unfortunately true

Albright was the only woman among the world leaders at the Denver Summit of the Eight in 1997

that there is plenty of room in the world for mediocre men, but there is no room for mediocre women.

It's important to have more than one woman in the room, because we can agree with each other. What men do is say, "As Bill said ...," which strengthens them. With another female voice in the room, we can act as a team.

I went to an all-girls high school, which I loved, and then to Wellesley, which continues to be a premier college. Being at a women's college meant that we had leadership roles and felt we could really run things. We worked very hard in the classroom, and our views were respected—you did not have to hide your light.

There were periods of my life when I was not sure if I would be able to carry out the desires that I had when I was in college. I had twin daughters when I was 24—they were born prematurely—and I initially stayed at home with them. But as much as I loved being a mother, I could not figure out why I had gone to college just to figure out how to get them in and out of the apartment or give them baths. I went through a time when I did not see any value in what I had done. I recently found a letter that I wrote at the time:

When I stepped off the platform after accepting my B.A. degree, I was confident that I was stepping into one or a series of interesting jobs. It was not the life of a career girl I was after, exactly. I was already up to my ears in plans for my wedding, three days hence. Still, I believed that in the natural course of events it would not be difficult to find interesting work that fit in with my political-science major. Two years later, I'm obsolete. Now it seems incomprehensibly naive for me to have thought a woman could compete on an equal basis with men for interesting jobs.

My desire had been to become a journalist. I worked on my college newspaper as an editor, and while my husband was in the Army I worked at a small newspaper in Missouri. When we moved back to Chicago, where my husband already had a job as

"It's important to have more than one woman in the room."

a journalist, we were having dinner with his managing editor, who said, "So what are you going to do, honey?" And I said, "I'm going to work at a newspaper."

He responded, "I don't think so. You can't work at the same paper as your husband because of labor regulations." I mentioned that there were three other papers in Chicago at the time, but he said, "You wouldn't want to compete with your husband." I know what you are thinking, and I know what I would say now. But at the time I simply saluted and went to find another life.

Other women were very critical of me when I was in graduate school, saying things like, "Wouldn't it be better if you were in the carpool line instead of the library?" And that my hollandaise sauce was not as good as theirs. And then, when I was working full time, they wondered what I was doing. That is where my statement originated—there is a special place in hell for women who do not help each other. We have to give each other space to be able to do what makes us feel that we are responsible and helping others, and doing what we want to be doing. We need to support each other in the lives that we have chosen. Men do not do that to each other, in terms of projecting their own ideas of weakness. Women need to take advantage of being women.

Albright served as U.S. ambassador to the U.N. from 1993 to 1997 and U.S. Secretary of State from 1997 to 2001.

Mary Barra

First woman to become CEO of a major car company

My first job was at a grocery store, where I learned about commitment to work. My father had an almost 40-year career at General Motors, and he encouraged me to pursue STEM. My mother taught me, Whatever you're going to do, do it well. My parents were raised during the Great Depression— they had a strong work ethic and believed in the American Dream.

People have a perception of the auto industry as being a traditional organization, but 20 years ago, there were leaders encouraging women to take challenging assignments. I have never felt that there was a glass ceiling at General Motors. Research has shown that women will look at a new role and say, "Well, I can do these five things, but there are two areas where I don't have experience, so maybe I shouldn't nominate myself." Men seem to say, "Hey, I can do five of the seven, I should definitely put myself forward!" I'm extremely proud of how many women we have in significant roles at General Motors, and it's work that started decades ago by developing a pipeline of people who were encouraged, mentored and given "stretch" assignments.

Women can put too much pressure on themselves, especially during transitions like having children. Sometimes you need to move into a different role, but it can be a building block for your career.

Barra joined GM when she was 18 and has been its CEO since 2014.

Patricia Bath

First person to invent and demonstrate laserphaco cataract surgery

"I wasn't seeking to be first.
I was just doing my thing, and
I wanted to serve humanity."

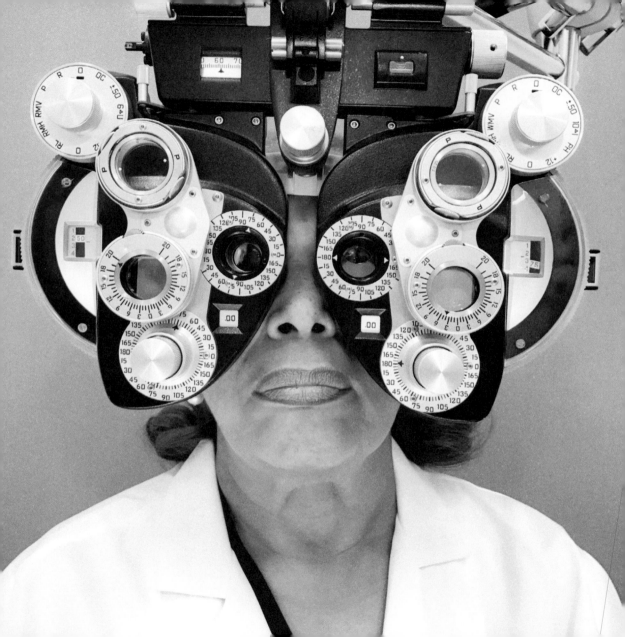

Sometimes even now when I'm told I was a "first," it comes as a surprise, because it's only through history that you understand that kind of thing. I didn't realize when I joined UCLA in 1974 that I was the first woman in the ophthalmology department. I simply wanted to be part of a great team at an incredible facility. I wasn't seeking to be first. I was just doing my thing, and I wanted to serve humanity along the way—to give the gift of sight.

I was always a curious child. I was given a chemistry set with a microscope, and I wanted to pretend-play and model myself after scientists. When we would play nurse and doctor, I didn't want to be forced to play the role of the nurse. I wanted to be the one with the stethoscope, the one who gave the injections, the one in charge. I have to thank my parents for having a gender-open household, for not setting limits.

I was in college between 1960 and 1964, so I did my marching, I did my protesting. When I was offered an office that was not equivalent to that of my male colleagues, I could have marched. But I felt it was more important to focus on the prize. One rainy, cold, lonely night in the lab, we had a donor eye. The laser was finely tuned, the optical fiber was in position and … *Eureka!* I knew that I had made a scientific breakthrough in removing cataracts.

I went to a prominent institute in Orange County and explained to the director what I had achieved. He said, "That's impossible. People have been trying to do that for years." He didn't believe me. A month or so later, after my patent had been granted and I published the findings, he was shocked. He wouldn't look me in the face.

In science, the evidence is the truth. I knew that my work would win the argument. And it did.

Bath was the first female African-American doctor to patent a medical device, the Laserphaco Probe, in 1988.

In 1974, Bath became the first woman in the ophthalmology department at UCLA

Elizabeth Blackburn

First woman to become president of the Salk Institute

"When somebody like me can be visible as a Nobel laureate, it says, Look, there is such a possibility."

I grew up in a small town in Tasmania, and I just loved animals. We had so many. At some point I counted in our house budgerigars, canaries, a dog, a cat, guinea pigs, rabbits, bantams and chickens. I liked looking at nature—trees and plants and ants and jellyfish. Living things just grabbed me, which turned into loving the idea of understanding how they work. I read a book about molecules and figured that that was the secret of life, and I determined that I was going to work with the molecules of life.

I was kind of an ornery character as a child—one of those kids who didn't like to be told to dress up or how to do drawings. I have a strong memory from kindergarten: I was drawing a big black locomotive, and my teacher said to me, "Don't use so much black." I was really mad. It was my locomotive—how dare anybody tell me how to draw it? I remember being angered that somebody would have another idea about how my locomotive ought to look. I was also a child who realized that I shouldn't make too much fuss—I was fairly well-behaved—but I had a streak of independence that I think put me in good stead for science as a career from that point onward.

I recall visiting the home of friends, and a man who was present asked me what I wanted to do one day. I said, "I'm going to be a scientist." And he said, "What's a nice girl like you doing going into science?" I was shocked and so mad that I didn't know what to say in response. So I kept my mouth shut, but I was all the more determined. In a way, I'm quite grateful to that man, because he made me realize that science was something I really wanted to do and that nobody was going to deflect me.

When I first began, in the 1970s, women in the life sciences were pretty unusual. Over the years, I started to notice that we had become less unusual. Then in the 1990s, I became the chair of a science department at a big medical school.

I remember going to the first meeting of all the chairs—clinical departments and basic sciences departments. I walked into the room, where I was the only woman, and I had this feeling that I was back in the 1970s. It struck me that, at that career level, women were much, much less in evidence and much, much less likely to have a high executive position than they were to be a scientist or even a physician for that matter. Biology is very complex, and it requires different depths of thought. If you cut out 50% of the world's minds from the problems of science, then you're losing a huge resource. You don't solve complex problems nearly as well.

Every woman thinks about balance in life. Work norms make it hard for you to be active in your career, which you love, and also manage the demands of family. Don't be afraid to ask for advice, because you'll find that there are possibilities that you didn't know about—career structures that will allow you to build in family time, or just practical advice. One is always surprised by how much people want you to succeed.

I sometimes see the glass ceiling in the number of women who get nominated for recognition. Men seem much more likely to be recognized than women, even if they are working on a team with a woman. So we have to say, Really? Is it because women contributed so little? There's plenty of evidence against that. When somebody like me can be visible as a Nobel laureate, it says, Look, there is such a possibility. There are only eight living women who have Nobel Prizes in the sciences, and I think we ought to be seen. If you're a young scientist and the Nobel laureates all look the same, you kind of get the sense that, Well, that's not something I can see myself as. Being visible is important.

Blackburn, president of the Salk Institute for Biological Studies since 2016, won the 2009 Nobel Prize in Physiology or Medicine for her DNA breakthroughs.

Ursula Burns

First black woman to run a *Fortune* 500 company

"The gender and
race differences
become a positive."

I became an engineer by accident, when I realized after taking a test as a junior in high school that I was actually good at math. I knew that I liked math and I thought I was O.K. at it, but after I took the PSAT, the guidance counselor came to me and said, "My God, you did a phenomenal job. You—you could be a mathematician." At that point I realized that what I thought was average was probably above average, and I hadn't even really been trying hard. If I put my shoulder into it, I probably would be even better.

I grew up in Manhattan in the late 1950s through the mid-'70s within about 10 blocks on the Lower East Side, in the Baruch housing projects. It was actually fun and good. I look back on it often, because if you see the neighborhood, there would be assumptions that we lived in squalor and fear and hunger. But there was none of that.

We started out in the tenements, and we kept moving up. We ended up in the housing projects, which were outstanding. If you went to them now, you would say, This is outstanding? But for us, the transitions were marked, and they were always a transition of improvement—from a tenement house to a little apartment in the projects to a bigger apartment in the projects. Those were all signs of progress for us.

It was my brother, my sister, my mother and me. If you asked my mother, she would probably say it was harder for her than for me. We had a very small community. We were poor. Our parents worked hard. Many of us—most of us—had a single parent. But we had a lot of control and structure. My mother struggled to make it O.K. for us, but we didn't have the Internet back then, so we didn't know how much other people had or how little we had.

Someone once characterized what they called "three strikes" against me. I thought it was an interesting thing to say, but I try not to characterize them as strikes: I was poor, I was black and I was female.

One of these—the poverty piece—you may be able to work your way out of.

> ## "You can perform as well as they can — or better."

But to have strikes for being female and black is a bad thing to think, and for people to say. You have no choice about those things. To say that by definition of who you are it is impossible or very unlikely for you to succeed, or to be considered a good person, or to be considered intelligent, or to have opportunities … That struck me when the person said it. I was not the first person they said it to, I'm sure. I have heard it before. But I've taken how unsettled I was and tried to change it. From that perspective, difference is generally better.

I grew up as an engineer in math and science, where it is mostly men. Mostly white men. All white men. All men. Again, difference is generally better. One of my strikes is the outcome of the other two. So you take the gender and the race differences and use them as a strength. They become a positive. You can perform as well as they can perform—or better—and you will be noticed. You have to have a continued focus and not bow to the many, many, many headwinds, but you can use them as an advantage. I say this to women all the time, particularly women who are trying to get into STEM.

For women and women of color, if you walk into a STEM environment, you will be the minority in the room. Everybody has their eye on your work. Instead of your differences becoming a burden, it should be an opportunity for you to distinguish yourself. That's what I turned those two "strikes" into.

Burns retired in 2017 as chair of Xerox, where she served as CEO from 2009 to 2016.

Candis Cayne

First transgender woman with a major role on prime-time TV

"I realized that if I was going
to perform and transition, I had
to do it in front of an audience."

I **have always been kind of a showboat.** I was never concerned with what other people thought of me, and I learned that from my parents. I would do crazy things when I was little, like fall in love with a pair of lederhosen. I would wear my little outfit every day to school, my socks up to my knees. I just kind of lived in an imaginary Candis world.

I grew up on Maui, where we moved when I was 10. I have a twin brother and two Waldorf-teaching parents who were always loving and supportive. And I've always been with a peer because I have a twin.

I've had the same mannerisms and acted the same way since I was a kid. My brother is my exact opposite—he was on all the sports teams, very intense and scholastic. He's just a brilliant person. We're like night and day. When we were growing up, he played with all his guy friends and rode dirt bikes; I'd be with my best friend Jenny and her Barbie collection, playing out crazy, wondrous, imaginative stories.

I knew right away that I was different from him, and that I was supposed to be more like him. But I didn't really care.

We have a pair of twin cousins, Teller and Tanya, who are a boy and a girl. My parents brought me and my brother to Sacramento to visit them, and I remember vividly the minute when I thought, I'm supposed to be like her. It was in late summer, when everything is kind of hazy and all the weeds are dry, and we were running through a field. I was having so much fun, and Tanya turned to me and I thought at that moment, What happened? Why wasn't I born like her?

At that age, you don't know what it means. There are no words for it, so you just kind of go on. But because my parents were so open and let me play with what I wanted and do what I wanted to do, I just was who I was.

I came out first, because I thought I was gay. As we all know now, gender and

"IT WAS LIKE
I COULD
BREATHE
FOR THE
FIRST TIME
IN MY LIFE."

sexuality are completely different. But because I didn't really know what trans was, I just assumed that I was gay. Five or six years later, I realized that I was trans. I wrote my parents each a letter and told them separately what I was going through. They booked tickets to New York City, where I was at the time, to make sure I was O.K. Their support has grown throughout the years.

Being trans is hard because you have to tell everybody in your life that you're making this big change. A lot of times what we want to do is close ourselves off, sit in a room, and start the transition that way. It's a lonely place to be, or it can be if you don't open yourself up and tell the people you love what's happening to you.

I remember deciding that what was best for me was to transition. I was kind of depressed and didn't understand why I was feeling that way. The only time I was really, truly happy was when I was performing. At the time, I lived on 14th Street and 9th Avenue in a teeny little room. I was at my makeup desk, I had two candles lit and they were glowing, and I saw this lilac aura around me. At that moment I realized, The reason I'm unhappy is because I'm not living in the right person. I don't feel whole. I wanted to grow old as a woman. I couldn't imagine growing old as a man. It didn't feel right. When I first started my hormone treatments, it was like I could breathe for the first time in my life. I felt true to myself.

I had known that I wanted to be an actor and a performer and a singer and a dancer and do it all, and the only way that I could do that was to do it onstage in the '90s in New York City and perform at the local gay bars. And I realized that if I was going to perform and transition, I had to do it onstage. I did that for two reasons. One, because I didn't want to start closing myself off, as I was saying earlier. And two, I wanted to educate the gay community. There were a few girls who were trans women, but not a lot. They were very segregated. I felt like we all needed to be one community. I would go to auditions and say, "I'm trans," and they'd say, "Oh, that's an interesting twist to the character." I tried to pitch myself, even though nobody really wanted to talk about it. I realized early on that I wasn't going to be able to change people's minds with facts and statistics and anger and yelling. I knew that one of my gifts was my charisma and being able to talk to people and be relatable. And I knew that once I got into a room with people who didn't quite understand who or what I was, they would embrace me because of my way of looking people in the face and saying, "This is what I need." I also knew that the more I did film and television and news shows and magazines, then my image, what I had to say and my kind of relatability, would be out there for the "normal" public to see.

Then I got a call from Patricia Field and she said, "I'm doing a pilot for this new television show, and I think you'd be great for the role." So I went and auditioned for *Dirty Sexy Money*. I had my Meryl Streep moment. And they took a chance on me. I'm sure they went to the network and had a back-and-forth, like, "Do we hire yet another cis woman to play this trans role? Do we hire a drag queen or a man to play this?" This was 10 years ago. It's a lot easier for Middle America to understand and to grasp now.

It was really the first time that a trans woman played a trans role for a recurring character—and the character had heart, she was an actual character that you could develop. Halfway through my first season, I went to an awards show, and they played a clip of me and Donald Sutherland doing a scene together. The whole room stood up and applauded. And I realized at that moment that this wasn't just about me wanting to be an actress; this was about moving the fabric of society forward.

Cayne, who started her career dancing in New York City, is known for her role on Dirty Sexy Money *and her appearances on* I Am Cait.

Eileen Collins

First woman to command a space shuttle

"I knew that all the women
in the program were mission
specialists—not pilots."

I **decided I wanted to be an astronaut** in fourth grade. I remember reading an article in *Junior Scholastic* about the Gemini program. I don't remember consciously feeling like I couldn't do it because they were all men and I was a young girl. I remember thinking, I'll just be a woman astronaut.

It wasn't until high school that I realized it would be impossible for me to be an astronaut as a woman. I remember very distinctly that I didn't tell anyone I wanted to be an astronaut because I didn't want anyone to tell me, "You can't do that." I didn't want to hear it. So I kept it inside. Even when I was in college and joined ROTC, I knew the end horizon was the astronaut program, but I never told anyone.

When I joined the Air Force, I was in the first class to have women go through pilot training at Vance Air Force Base, in Enid, Okla. I think there were 450 pilots on that base, and we were the first four women. The Air Force was testing whether women could succeed as military pilots. We obviously were living in a fishbowl—everyone knew who we were, our personal business, our test scores and our flight performance. My philosophy was to be the best pilot I could be—to stay focused, not engage or get involved in social things or anything that wasn't directly contributing to the mission. It was important for us to excel in training and for the test program to succeed. If the first women did poorly, that could have caused the cancellation of the program.

I must have been on the base for two days when I was checking out the commissary wearing my flight suit. A woman in a flight suit was a strange sight in those days. The woman behind the register said, "Are you one of those new women pilots?" I said yes. She looked at me and said, "The wives don't want you here." I was thinking—the guys don't want us here, the wives don't want us here. I felt horrible. So I asked her why. She said, "They don't want you going cross-country with their husbands!" This frank interaction helped me see our situation through other people's eyes. I wanted the women pilots to integrate successfully, so I made it a point to get to know the wives.

While at Vance, in 1978, the first class of space-shuttle astronauts visited for three days of parachute training. I never met any of them, but everybody was talking about them. That's when I decided to apply to the space-shuttle program as soon as I was eligible. I knew that all the women in the program were mission specialists, not pilots. I also knew that to be a shuttle pilot you had to be a test pilot. So I applied to test-pilot school. That's when I knew I could be the first woman shuttle pilot, because there were very few women ahead of me in the pipeline in the Air Force or the Navy.

In 1990 I learned that I was going to pilot the space shuttle when Duane Ross at NASA called me. He handed me off to [commander of the Apollo 16 mission] John Young. I asked, "Am I going to be a pilot or a mission specialist?" He said, "You're going to be a pilot. You will be the first woman pilot of the space shuttle." John Young is one of my heroes; he not only walked on the moon but was the first person to land the space shuttle. I hung up the phone. I didn't feel like jumping up and down or partying. I felt a sense of relief, a huge sense of calmness.

After my first mission, I was visiting a group of women at Kennedy Space Center. One woman said, "Thank you for doing what you are doing, because it makes guys respect us more." That hit me between the eyes. I thought, Why didn't I think of that before? This isn't just about me. This is really a big, big deal.

I advise others to take on challenges, even if you think they are too hard, even if you think you might fail. When you become an old person and look back on your life you may say, "I wish I had tried that"—you don't want to be in that position. Give yourself challenges that are exciting, and be available to help others. There is no better feeling than helping someone else.

Collins became an astronaut in 1991 and served as a pilot or commander on four spaceflights before retiring from NASA in 2006.

Kellyanne Conway

First woman to run a winning presidential campaign

I grew up an only child in a very unconventional household that contained my mother, her mother and two of my mother's unmarried sisters. Four Italian Catholic women. I call them South Jersey's version of the Golden Girls, wearing the housecoats with the snaps and everything. I was taught to be self-possessed, respectful, decorous, patient, kind and generous—wonderful, positive attributes that serve you well in life. But I was also taught to be a little self-denying, even as some women would find that shocking, wondering why is that a positive attribute?

To be part of a team or a household where other people's interests and needs share space with yours requires skills best formed early in life, particularly for an only child who is otherwise spoiled. It has served me well, whether at my company or working in the legal and consulting professions, and certainly in managing Donald Trump's presidential campaign and working in the White House.

I was taught to be a very strong, independent and freethinking woman without ever hearing the words *feminist* or *Republican* or *liberal.* I appreciate that so much, to have not been fed labels and taught definitions, but instead to have been given the foundation upon which to develop my own strengths to my best and highest use throughout my educational, professional and maternal endeavors.

Conway founded her consulting firm, the Polling Company, in 1995 and became Trump's final campaign manager in 2016. She is counselor to the President.

Mo'ne Davis

**First girl to pitch a shutout and win a game
in a Little League World Series**

"When the other team
saw me face the batter,
they were shocked."

I **started playing baseball** when I was about 7 or 8. I had been playing football with my cousin and his friends. We were tackling each other, and I was throwing spirals about 30 yards, which is really good for a little girl. My coach gave me his phone number on this little sticky note and told me to give it to my mom. She was very hesitant—she didn't want me to be playing sports, and she didn't know it was a boys' team. Once she found out, she was like, "No." But somehow we convinced her, and now I think she enjoys it. She enjoys watching me play.

The first time I walked out onto the field to pitch, the other team said I wasn't going to be good—that they were going to win. They were telling jokes; the parents were laughing. My team and I knew they could laugh all they wanted to ... When they saw me face the first batter, they were shocked. You didn't hear anything from that side of the field. It was fun for us and not fun for them. Just because I'm a girl doesn't mean anything. I kept getting better, and the game got better.

When you throw a fastball and know it's good, that you can control it, or you throw a first strike and they swing and miss or can't swing at all—it's a good feeling. I can't describe it. It's like taking a bite in a really good slice of pizza. Once you throw that first pitch or take that bite, everything else is plain and simple, and you enjoy it.

I'm kind of used to striking out guys now, but when I first started, a lot of people didn't think I was good. So when I struck them out, it just changed everyone's perspective and how people went into the game. I guess word got around the league to beware of the Monarchs: "They have this girl pitcher. Don't get too cocky or anything, just play your game." We sent a good message for our team.

The Monarchs finished the Little League World Series in 2014 with two wins. Davis, now 16, has turned her attention to basketball.

After her historic shutout, Davis was named Best Breakthrough Athlete at the 2015 ESPYs

Ellen DeGeneres

First person to star as an openly gay character on prime-time TV

"It was everything that I wanted it to be ... And it was everything that I feared."

When I first started doing stand-up, I was writing from the perspective of a human being, observing how we all act—it had nothing to do with a female perspective. It was just a human one. I don't know if that's because I'm gay and I just didn't really identify with men and women being so different, but I didn't consciously think, I'm not doing female material.

Comedy is a very political world. You're supposed to work your way up, especially in San Francisco. There was one night in particular when I was the headliner. I had just moved there and had just been named Showtime's "Funniest Person in America." There were two guys opening for me who were angry that I was headlining and had been on Showtime. No one knew that I was gay necessarily. But their stuff was very homophobic, and it slammed women in every kind of way. By the time I got onstage, it was a very angry, testosterone-filled crowd. And I just bombed. I was doing a phone call to God. God's talking, and I'm listening—there are spaces for people to yell out. The entire front row of guys turned their chairs around and faced the audience. Everyone laughed. The whole audience was against me. So I walked off the stage.

One of the guys came back onstage and said, "That was the funniest person in America, ladies and gentlemen, the funniest per—" He kept saying it over and over. It was a horrible, horrible night, a night when I thought I would never do comedy again. I don't know where those guys are now, but they didn't get the Medal of Freedom.

I didn't really come into my own power and understanding of who I am until probably the last 10 years. I was very shy. I was insecure. I needed to feel liked and loved, which is why most people go into this business. I wasn't ever motivated to say, "I'll show them." I kept doing comedy out of love—when it works, there's nothing better than making people laugh. There's no better feeling.

Everything in my life is exactly perfect in the good things, and especially in the bad things—they made me who I am, and they've made me a more compassionate person.

Before DeGeneres had her own show, she was named Showtime's "Funniest Person in America"

So I wouldn't change anything in my life, including the way I came out. I was carrying this fear around that if people found out that I was gay, I would lose everything. I didn't want to have a secret. Straight people don't say, "My private business is my private business." They don't not answer the question. There was something wrong that I was so filled with shame about my sexuality.

When I came out, it made sense that the character on my sitcom *Ellen* would come out too. I thought it was a really interesting story to tell. To have Laura Dern play my girlfriend, and to have Oprah Winfrey be my therapist. I made a call to Oprah and said, "I'm going to come out on my show. Would you please play my therapist?" It was the greatest thing in the world. It was everything that I wanted it to be, as far as the way the show turned out. And it was everything that I feared that it would be, which is that I would lose my show and my career. And it was also the greatest thing that could have happened, because it sent me on a different trajectory, and here I am now.

Everybody said, "You'll destroy this whole show." And I was like, "Yeah, but it's my life." I was warned by my publicist at the time. I was warned by Disney. I was warned by everybody. But there's nothing better than realizing that everybody knows exactly who I am. I wasn't trying to be political. I wasn't trying to do anything other than get that out of the way so I didn't have to worry about hiding.

It was a long process trying to sell [my current] show. There were station managers who thought, No one's going to watch a gay woman in daytime because everyone at home is a housewife with kids. But then we did sell it. To be sitting here 14 years later ... I wouldn't have believed it. All I did was get back to what I started out doing, which is wanting to make people happy.

DeGeneres, an Emmy-winning TV host and comedian, has hosted her eponymous talk show since 2003.

"I WOULDN'T CHANGE ANYTHING, INCLUDING THE WAY I CAME OUT."

Gabby Douglas

**First American gymnast to win solo and team
all-around gold medals at one Olympics**

"My mom always used to
say, 'Inspire a generation.'"

My first introduction to gymnastics was through my older sister Arielle. She used to be a gymnast, and I saw her doing gymnastics drills. I wanted to do what she was doing, so she taught me how to do my first cartwheel. My mom says that by the end of the week, I was teaching myself one-armed cartwheels and aerials and my sister was like, "You need to put this kid in gymnastics."

I was always an adrenaline junkie. When I was 3, I would climb up the doorframes on walls and just sit there. From a young age, I did it for fun. I never knew it was going to be something that I did—my career. I just fell in love with gymnastics.

At about age 9, I realized, Hey, I want to take this seriously—I want to pursue the Olympic path. I was always in front of cameras at meets, so I was used to the public eye. But the Olympic stage is different. The Games teach you to act a certain way, to be disciplined, to tweak this and tweak that. They teach you to be a mature young lady, and you grow up fast. I never knew what to expect.

The last Olympic Games were pretty rough for me. I was not expecting a whole bunch of criticism on every single thing I did. Sure, I was expecting a little here and there because I had dealt with it in 2012, but I was caught off guard by the extent of it. Even though you have to perform, you also have to look your best, but sometimes you don't have makeup in your bag, or you sweat, or you don't have a brush. Some gymnasts don't wear makeup, and people say, "Oh, she looks rough!" Makeup to me is part of being in character—like a bow in your hair. And then of course people say, "Why do you have makeup on? This is a competition, not a beauty pageant! You don't need makeup, you look pretty without it." You can't please everybody, so just do your normal.

When I started this journey, I never knew what it actually took to get to the

Olympics. I thought it was: Train. Make it on the team. Go to the Olympics. I had to sacrifice a normal kind of life for gymnastics, but I didn't mind. The sacrifices meant moving from Virginia Beach to Iowa, getting a different coach. I sacrificed my privacy and my life. Gymnastics is what I was going to eat, breathe and sleep. I lived with a host family. I was so close with my own family, so that was a huge change for me. I'm the baby of my family. But when I went to Iowa, I was a big sister. How does a young person help even younger ones? So, it was different, and I missed my family a lot. It also felt like déjà vu—doing everything the same, every day, for 14 years is grueling. It takes a lot to be an Olympic athlete. You have to be amazing, and you have to work hard. You may have a talent, but the people who work harder than you will surpass you.

Throughout my career, a lot of people have doubted me. When someone tells you that you can't do it, especially when there are multiple people, you start to believe it, and you don't believe in yourself. It took me about 10 years to figure out how great I was at gymnastics. You have to believe that you're good enough.

In 2011, I strained my hamstring and my hip flexor, though in training I had still been doing well. But when I went out onto the competition floor, I fell seven times. It was the national championships, and I was on TV. Seven times?! It was so embarrassing. My mom told me, "That's what a winner is—when you fall and you get right back up and you don't quit." But I said, "I don't think I want to try until next year." My coaches were like, "Just try out for the world championships," and I was like, "I don't think I'm going to try." It's awful—the worst thing ever— when you're so talented and you believe that you can do something, but fear holds you back. It's torment.

But I went to the world championships and I got a team gold, and it was a great experience. The coach I was working with at the time told me, "All right, when we get back to the gym, we're going to get it." He made me sweat, and I love it, I love hard work—it means I'm accomplishing something.

Then 2012 came around, and I got invited to do the American Cup. I was a different person, a different gymnast. Everyone was just like, "Dang! Who is this girl?"

It was that drive, it was "I'm not going to be embarrassed again. I have a talent and I'm going to use it."

It's important to have strong female individuals to look up to—because everyone struggles. I love Serena Williams. People can say mean things to her, and she literally is just like, Nah, I'm still going to do whatever it is. You don't get to tell me. She plays with the criticism. It's awesome, and I want to start doing that. People can be so negative and so mean, but you just make it fun, and bring them back to love.

And I have learned from my mom and my sisters to always fight, always, and to never give up, no matter what the odds look like. My mom has sacrificed her whole life for me to achieve mine, and I'm so grateful for that. Sometimes parents try to live a dream through their kids, but it has to be the kid's choice, and the kid's passion.

My mom always used to say, "Inspire a generation." It's one thing when you say it, but I never thought that I would be a trailblazer and that people would draw inspiration from my story. When that happened, we were like, "Whoa!" To be a role model to these young girls … I love it. It's like I'm a big sister.

Douglas won three gold medals at the 2012 and 2016 Olympic Games and helped Team USA win gold at the 2011 and 2015 world championships.

In 2012, Douglas became the first African-American gymnast to win the all-around gold medal

Rita Dove

First black U.S. poet laureate

"Raising hackles means you're not being ignored; you're pushing the conversation forward."

When I began writing about ordinary, middle-class African Americans' lives—especially in *Thomas and Beulah,* my third book of poetry, which deals with a solid lifelong marriage devoid of extraordinary drama—I was keenly aware that such experiences had not received their due in contemporary poetry. Whatever I pursue—writing poetry or teaching or speaking in public—I want to be excited by the challenge, curious about where life might next lead me. If I'm not both thrilled and terrified at the prospect of stepping out into unknown territory that might teach me something new, then something is wrong, then I'm too complacent.

Receiving the Pulitzer Prize was like having a spotlight turned on. Although I had published several books, I did not expect much in the way of media attention. Poets aren't used to a lot of fanfare, particularly in this country; rarely are they thrust upon a national stage. And yet suddenly there was a growing audience reading my work and listening to me. As an artist, it was immensely gratifying to see how these stories dealing with intimate moments in the lives of ordinary people, those who'll never make it into the history books, found resonance on a national level and beyond, regardless of race or gender.

Being chosen as our nation's first African-American poet laureate was a further challenge. I felt called to speak to the importance of poetry, the humanities and the arts in our lives. It meant serving as a lightning rod for the American people in their quest for those truths that neither politics nor psychotherapy could address. And indeed, I was immediately inundated with letters from total strangers who were eager to tell me about the first time they had encountered poetry and how it had changed their lives. Many of these accounts began with "I don't know much about poetry" and were often followed by a passionate description of a particular poem. These confessions impressed and saddened me. Because many of my correspondents had had no exposure to poetry as children in school, they were afraid of sounding "stupid" and being deemed unworthy of discussing this "elite" art form. Yet this trepidation could be overcome through the impact of a single poem, with the rapt reader finding emotional support and solace for his or her soul.

When I was asked to be the sole editor of *The Penguin Anthology of 20th Century American Poetry,* I encountered another glass ceiling. Anthologies are often done by teams. For a lone individual (and an African-American woman at that!) to be given the responsibility of choosing who would represent American poetry for the entire past century was unheard of. Producing a mainstream anthology in a field dominated by a mostly white male establishment was a daunting task, and I took it very seriously. That there was some pushback came as no surprise—but raising hackles means you're not being ignored; you're pushing the conversation forward.

Although I am not a confrontational person by nature, racism and sexism are still very much alive, and whenever I encounter prejudice, I tackle the issues and move on, refusing to be sidetracked by hate or bitterness. When I was a young poet, my work was considered "slight" by some male critics. The sexist undertone was undeniable, though difficult to corroborate. These things are subtle. For example, during my 20s and 30s there was an unspoken rule that if you wore makeup or gave a poetry reading in a dress, you weren't considered a serious artist—a variation on brain vs. beauty, that ancient claim that pretty girls are airheads and smart girls are plain. It sounds so trivial nowadays, yet the implications could be profound—or so I was told. To hell with it, was my response. This is who I am. I still wear skirts to readings. And I still like my lipstick!

Dove, who won the Pulitzer Prize for her poetry in 1987, served as U.S. poet laureate from 1993 to 1995.

Ann Dunwoody

First woman to rise to four-star general in the U.S. military

"I didn't look at myself as
a woman in uniform. I looked
at myself as a soldier."

I **was a tomboy.** I loved sports. I was going to be a coach and phys-ed teacher, so joining the Army never really occurred to me, even though I came from this incredible Army family background, with four generations of West Pointers: my brother, my dad, my dad's dad and my great-grandfather. My older sister became the Army's third female helicopter pilot.

During my junior year in college at SUNY Cortland, the Army was recruiting women into the Corps after Vietnam. If you qualified, you got a commission as a second lieutenant, a two-year commitment and they paid you $500 a month during your senior year in college—a lot of money back then.

So I said, "I can stand on my head for two years." I signed up knowing full well that it was just going to be a two-year detour from my coaching and teaching profession.

And then two years turned into five turned into 10 and turned into 38.

My dad was always my hero; a funny, smart leader with a chest full of medals. But I realized later in life that my mom was the real hero, and if I could be more like her, I would be a better soldier and a better leader. So I had a dad who was a mentor and a mom who was the human dimension, who said, "Do the right thing for the right reason and take care of people."

When they started integrating women into the regular Army, I was into my first year and a half in the military, and that's when I had the opportunity to go to Airborne School. For the first time, women could have the same career path as their male counterparts.

We took advantage because our challenge was not to let the institution keep us in those cook and nurse slots. I wanted to be a platoon leader—and not a female platoon leader. I wanted to be a platoon leader for men and women.

Throughout my career, I found that we want the best and the brightest on our team, whether you're male or female. The best athletes, the best shooters. And when

In 1992, Dunwoody became the first female battalion commander for the 82nd Airborne Division

you can run faster than the guys, when you can do more pushups, they don't look at you and say, "Oh, we don't want you on our team." They go, "Wow! We want you on our team because we need the best."

I put leaders in three categories. You have people who are advocates and are impressed with you. These leaders believed in my potential, and they influenced the institutional process to give me opportunities that I would never have had. The next category are patronizers. And you all know them. You might be able to make them into believers but most of them are threatened by either who you are or what you can do. And then there are people who I call detractors that just don't like you: "This is a man's world, we don't need you in here." But I think many of them can become believers once you're on their team, and you demonstrate that you're as capable, committed, dedicated and professional as anyone else.

I've never worked for a woman. I've only worked for men who either believed in me or didn't. Fortunately, most of them were advocates for me, and the others I tried to make believers by not lowering my standards. I didn't look at myself as a woman in uniform. I looked at myself as a soldier.

I was unprepared for the enormity of my nomination to four-star general. I received duffel bags full of mail and many emails from men, women, children and veterans around the world saying how happy they were that this day had finally arrived.

And one of the Reserve NCOs who worked with me sent me a letter that said, "General Dunwoody, I'm so proud! I can finally tell my three daughters that they can be anything they want to be, including a four-star general in the Army."

Dunwoody, who served nearly four decades in the U.S. military, rose to become a four-star general in 2008 and retired in 2012 as commander of the Army Materiel Command.

"WE WANT
THE BEST
AND THE
BRIGHTEST,
MALE OR
FEMALE."

Ava DuVernay

**First black woman to direct a film
nominated for a Best Picture Oscar**

"It's about making sure we
push against tokenism and
vain attempts at diversity."

Regarding "the glass ceiling," I think there have been cracks made by women who can get close enough to hit it with the weapon of their presence. But I'm mostly bolstered by folks who create their own ceilings. I'm less interested in banging down the door of some man who doesn't want me there. I'm more about building my own house. Certainly, I sit here privileged, after decades of women who have done it and have allowed me to think in this way. I am grateful to them.

For anyone who is working in a house that was not built for them, at times it is not particularly welcoming. There are ways to work within a system. There are like-minded people who understand the power of their privilege and understand that they can open up opportunities for others. But largely not. So, it's about making sure we push against tokenism and vain attempts at diversity, and push for different points of view to be centered, valued and seen.

As a publicist, I was on sets where no one knew my name. My work wasn't valued beyond the product. So as a filmmaker, I like to know about my crew members. The experience of making something embeds itself in the image. When I watch a film, I can tell when it's been made with no joy. I try to have joy in my filmmaking.

If the person who gets to tell the story is always one kind of person, if the dominant images that we see throughout our lifetimes, our mothers' lifetimes, our grandmothers' lifetimes, have been dominated by one kind of person, and we take that? We internalize it. We drink it in, as true, as fact. The images in our minds that make up our memories are all told by one kind of person, one kind of background. It shouldn't be this way. That is a deficit to us. A deficit to the culture.

DuVernay directed Selma, *an Oscar nominee for Best Picture, and* 13th, *an Oscar nominee for Best Documentary Feature.*

"I'M BOLSTERED BY FOLKS WHO CREATE THEIR OWN CEILINGS."

Sylvia Earle

**First woman to become chief scientist of the
U.S. National Oceanic and Atmospheric Administration**

"When I was in high school,
science seemed like a guy
thing, but I loved it."

The first time I went underwater, I was 3 years old, and I was knocked over by a wave. The ocean got my attention. Years later I had a chance to breathe compressed air underwater, through a copper diving helmet. Our next-door neighbor in Florida was a sponge diver, and my older brother and the sponge diver's son conspired to "borrow" the equipment: the helmet, a compressor and a hose that connected the compressed air. I just wore a bathing suit and went barefoot, so my feet kept floating up. That was my first experience. A year later, in 1953, I used scuba for the first time, with two words of instruction: "Breathe naturally." It was glorious—I could get acquainted with the fish and be free of any connection to the surface. It was like flying. What I love about the ocean is you never know whom you're going to see or what you're going to do, but it's always going to be good. It's always going to be a thrill.

When I was in high school, science was not a particularly attractive field for many young women. It seemed like a guy thing, but I loved it. I wanted to be an ecologist, somebody who looked at how the whole system works. When I began college, I was often the only woman in a class.

I came along at a time when women were just beginning to be accepted as competent scientists and engineers. Having women on ships was not a particularly welcomed thing. The U.S. Navy took a long time to allow women. Now there are women captains, and you finally see the idea of brain over brawn, even on commercial ships. It was and is about, Can you do the job? Are you able? Can you handle this machinery? But that wasn't always the way.

The cultural bias is what it is. Men and women are different, and the society of men as leaders has predominated the society in which I came along. It's still very much there, but it's getting better. Women are every bit as intellectually competent as our male counterparts.

Earle set the record for deepest untethered dive when she explored at a depth of 1,250 ft.

On one of my first oceanographic expeditions, in 1964, I did not yet have my Ph.D. (In fact, it took me 10 years to earn a Ph.D. because I got married and had two of my three children along the way.) I was the only woman with 70 men for six weeks at sea in the Indian Ocean. I had never been west of the Mississippi River before I went halfway around the world to the Indian Ocean. But then the headline on an interview I did, which ran in the Mombasa *Daily Times,* was "Sylvia Sails Away With 70 Men. But She Expects No Problems." It was my first real interaction with the press. I don't know what problems they thought I might have. To my mind the goals were: keep a sense of humor; don't expect favors; do what you're there to do as a scientist. In an atmosphere where other people may expect you to be treated differently, you try not to be treated differently. I took being a scientist very seriously. I still do.

Later, I was a scientist at Harvard when I noticed a paper on the bulletin board asking if anyone would be interested in living underwater as a scientist for two weeks in the U.S. Virgin Islands. The idea was to come up with a project that would be reviewed by scientists at the Smithsonian Institution and sponsored by the Department of the Interior. No mention was made about having to be a guy, but it was clear that no one expected women to apply. But some of us did. And the rest is history, if you will.

The idea of men and women living underwater together wasn't going to fly, but they allowed us to have a women's team, and I was the leader. That put me in the hot seat again. We attracted attention from all around the world. The men who did this, they were called aquanauts. The women, we were aqua-babes, aqua-chicks, aqua-naughties. But we didn't care what they called us, as long as we had a chance to go.

We had a wonderful time. We spent a lot of time in water, day and night. I'd been diving, of course. I had more than 1,000 hours at that point, but just in and out— 20 minutes or sometimes only five or 10 minutes at a time. Here we had 24 hours

"Women are every bit as competent as men."

a day for two weeks, in and out at our will. Once we were underwater, it was just freedom. We wanted to be out there getting acquainted with the fish on their terms.

People asked us all kinds of silly questions—Did we use a hair dryer? Did we wear lipstick?—but we used that opening to explain the nature of the ocean: how beautiful it is, how vulnerable it is. How, even back then, there was evidence that what we were doing to it was causing problems. It wasn't pristine—there had already been a reduction in some of the fish that we would normally see on a coral reef, for example—but compared with today, it was glorious because of the variety. Today 90% of many of those fish are just gone.

Our time down there was breathtaking. It was just beautiful. The fish weren't afraid of us, even though they'd seen primates in the water before—people there to spear them, for instance. But we weren't there to kill them, so with us, when we behaved ourselves and treated them the way they liked to be treated, with dignity and respect, they were friendly. The fish were curious about us. That's when I thought, Do unto the fish as you would have fish do unto you.

And when you treat them like that, it's amazing what you can see. It's true when you deal with humans that way too.

Earle is president and chair of Mission Blue, an organization that advocates for legal protection and conservation of the world's oceans.

Aretha Franklin

First woman to be inducted into the Rock and Roll Hall of Fame

"I didn't think my songs would become anthems for women. But I'm delighted."

The first songs I sang in church were "Jesus Be a Fence Around Me" and "I Am Sealed." I was around 8 or 9. My dad asked me to sing that day. I didn't want to sing in front of an audience. But he heard the possibilities and he continued to encourage me, and thank God he did. Singing at a concert vs. singing in the church is like singing no place else, really. You have an ethereal feeling there. The house of God is the house of God. But all music is motivating, inspiring, transporting.

I didn't think my songs would become anthems for women. But I'm delighted. Women probably immediately feel compassion and relate to the lyrics. We can all learn a little something from each other, so whatever people can take and be inspired by where my music is concerned is great.

When we recorded "Respect" and "Natural Woman" in the studio, everyone—the musicians and singers—stood up. We were on air, really happy about the takes. My producer at the time, Jerry Wexler, a VP of Atlantic Records, said, "Let's wait until tomorrow night this time. If we feel the same way tomorrow, if we're still standing on air about it, we probably have a hit." He would still be walking on air to this day.

Women have done well in the music industry, with the exception of those male bastions: the executive offices. We have not had a female executive run any major label in the U.S. or anyplace else that I know of right now.

My cousin once told me not to take other people so seriously. You know, she was right. Especially where men are concerned. And I don't think women need to do anything other than what they're doing right now, and that's moving forward. Moving to the forefront. Moving into the executive offices. Moving into the areas that men have held captive. We're coming.

Franklin has won 18 Grammy Awards.

"WE CAN ALL LEARN A LITTLE SOMETHING FROM EACH OTHER."

Melinda Gates

First woman to give away more than $40 billion

"The plight of women was
a rallying call I couldn't turn
away from."

My dad worked in the aerospace and aeronautics industry, and on a lot of those early Apollo missions. He made sure that my sister and I would watch the missions at night when they took off. We would often hear around the dinner table stories about his teams and what they were working on. He talked about the women he was recruiting and said that when he had these women mathematicians on his team, his whole team was better. Now we have statistics that show that teams and corporations are better if you have diverse points of view. I got lucky—I had a dad and a mom telling me I could be anything I wanted to be in the world. They said that very consistently to me and my siblings. If your dad believes in you, that's important to young girls. If your dad thinks you can be good at math and science, good at business, good at anything, it lifts your confidence and your self-esteem.

Men speaking up and saying "I want women on my project" makes a difference. Or sticking up for a woman in a meeting and saying, "She just said what you repeated for her. It didn't need repeating." Or making sure that when a role opens, women know they should put their name in the hat and that they're qualified for the job. It's important for men and women to do that, but in some ways it's even more important that men do it, because men are in more positions of power.

In our foundation work, I originally thought that the women's issues were the soft issues. And I was just wrong about that. I saw that only women were talking about these issues, and I'm used to working in very male-oriented fields, right? Computer science and math and all these places I've been. So I thought, Well, I'm not going to just talk about what the women are talking about—I'm going to talk about what the men are talking about.

But as I was out in the field with families, I realized the reason women were talking about women's issues was that no one else was championing them. The world wasn't actually putting resources behind women's health in the right way. In children's health and adolescent health, you don't just invest in the boy child, you invest in the girl as well. I was hearing over and over and over again about the plight of women. And I thought, Who's giving voice to them? Who's bringing their issues to the world stage? Who's saying we need to make investments in contraceptives, which they were asking me for? It was a rallying call I couldn't turn away from.

At the same time I was raising three young children—a daughter, a son and another daughter. I thought, especially for my oldest daughter who at the time was just entering adolescence, if I'm telling her she should use her voice or speak about what she believes in, I need to be role-modeling that in the world. And I wasn't. Over time I decided that if I had this platform of the foundation, I actually needed to use my voice.

I've come to learn that, as in business, we haven't had good data in philanthropy. We're getting it now. But even when the world says they invest in data, they don't invest in data around women. And if we don't invest in collecting statistics about women, we don't know how and where to act. So I'm making sure that we take these business principles to women's issues. Then we can get the world to invest.

I wouldn't say that the world sees women's issues as soft issues anymore. If I'm at the U.N., there are many Prime Ministers speaking about girls' education these days, because they want their whole society to work. If girls participate in economic opportunities, it'll change their countries. We need to unlock the potential for girls and women to let them fully participate and be who they are in the world. And we'll see amazing things because of it.

Gates, who has degrees in computer science and economics as well as business administration, worked at Microsoft from 1987 to 1996. She is a co-chair of the Bill & Melinda Gates Foundation.

Selena Gomez

First person to reach 100 million followers on Instagram

My mom did a lot of theater growing up. So I think it was instinctual for me to perform. I loved being able to make people laugh, and if anyone was sad, I didn't like it. I always tried to make people feel good, to feel something. So whenever I would see my mom perform, I thought, Maybe I'll have the chance to do that one day. I would use my entire neighborhood as my stage.

When I started working as a child, my mom was the person in my life who helped guide me. I understood that acting was a job, that I would have fun, that I would enjoy it—and that if I didn't enjoy it anymore, that I should stop doing it. I also had school to do. That's the base of how I grew up. There were moments when I had to be like an adult, but when I was on set, I still felt like a kid.

I am glad I grew up in the time that I did. I think it's really hard to be a kid now, especially with social media. I can't imagine what it would be like to grow up with that. It's already difficult to get up every day and just feel good about yourself without seeing the highlights of everyone else's life. That's why I like being vulnerable with my fans on social media. I like that they've seen my mistakes. I try to use that as a way to connect with them. That's all I can do. I hope that they know that strength doesn't mean that you have to put on a facade. Strength is being vulnerable.

Gomez began her career on the Disney Channel and is an actor and singer.

Nikki Haley

First Indian-American woman to be elected governor

"I wanted to be mayor of Bamberg one day—that was as high as I could see."

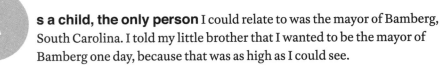

A **s a child, the only person** I could relate to was the mayor of Bamberg, South Carolina. I told my little brother that I wanted to be the mayor of Bamberg one day, because that was as high as I could see.

We were the only Indian family in town. Nobody knew who we were or what we were. My father wore a turban, my mother wore a sari, and we were different. But my parents always said that the things that make you different make you special. When we would come home complaining that we had been teased, my mom would say, "Your job is not to show people how you're different. It's to show them how you're similar." I grew up trying to show people what we have in common.

Every person has war stories. Things happen in your life that change you and challenge you, and they're uncomfortable, but when you get through them, you realize that they are the reason you are the way that you are.

When I was little, everybody's child was in the Little Miss Bamberg pageant, so my mom put my sister and me in the pageant. But during the pageant, they disqualified us. My mom said, "Why are you disqualifying us?" They said, "Well, we have to have a black queen, and we have to have a white queen, and we don't know where to put your daughters. If we put them on either side, that side would be angry." They gave me a beach ball and sent me on my way. But my mom said, "Well, at least let her do her talent." So I sang, "This land is your land, this land is my land," to everyone before I got disqualified.

At the time, I didn't know exactly how wrong it was, but I did want to know why I couldn't be part of the group. Now I look back and I realize that labels really mattered. That's why I try so hard not to talk about labels now. At the end of the day, we're so much more similar than we are different.

Haley served as South Carolina's governor from 2011 to 2017. She is the U.S. ambassador to the United Nations.

"WE'RE
SO MUCH
MORE
SIMILAR
THAN
WE ARE
DIFFERENT."

Carla Hayden

First woman and first African American to be Librarian of Congress

"Eighty-five percent of the library workforce is female but men are in most directorships."

B *right April* **by Marguerite de Angeli** was how I first learned about library fines. I was an 8-year-old girl going to P.S. 96 in Queens, and there was a storefront branch right across the street.

I don't remember who put that book in my hand, but somebody knew that a little girl who was brown and had pigtails needed a book that reflected her. I saw myself in a book and that will never leave me. I love that book to this day.

When you grow up in a family that was devoted to education and where books were important, and then you see yourself reflected in something that's important, it gives you a sense of "There I am. There I am." It's so important that children see themselves, but also are exposed to the world. Books can be mirrors and windows, we like to say.

In terms of being the Librarian of Congress, it's important that a woman is in the position. Librarianship is one of the four "feminized professions." Eighty-five percent of the workforce is female but men are in most of the directorships and management positions. So to have a woman Librarian of Congress is just as significant as race in terms of diversity.

Librarians have a strong stereotype. When you see *It's a Wonderful Life,* and Jimmy Stewart is looking for Donna Reed at the end and she's coming out of a library . . . very strong stereotype. When people think "librarian," they say, "Oh, must be kind of dull." In commercials when they want to show that a product is really snappy, a librarian tastes the gum and goes wild. That's what people think about the librarian. To have the profession represented by someone who is somewhat culturally diverse, with a short haircut, shows that librarians can be cool. I think it will help with our recruitment.

In Baltimore, the library was at the epicenter of the unrest in 2015. It had been a refuge for that community. An opportunity center—expungement classes, flu shots, people online applying for jobs. When that library was not only protected during the unrest and then was open the next day, that Tuesday morning—I'll never forget it—at 10 o'clock, there were people waiting to get inside. Not only for refuge and a place to connect but there was, for instance, a young man who was so relieved that we were open so he could fill out applications online. That Thursday, he came back and said he had three nibbles. That's what a library in a community can mean.

When I first started library studies, it was in the mid-'70s, and there was a lot going on culturally. I was in school with people from all walks of life. We were very idealistic. There were very few men. After I graduated, I was asked to be on a panel with a few other classmates, who had also gotten jobs, to talk to the incoming graduate students. There were two female colleagues and then a gentleman, who … let's just say he was not the brightest star in the class. I was a children's librarian. One of my other colleagues was in cataloguing and the other was doing reference. This young man had on a suit and a tie, and he was a manager already. I think we all collectively kind of looked surprised that he was in this position, and we kind of did a "Gawww, gee! How did *that* happen?"

Over time, as I had more management experience, when I was for instance selected to be the director of the Enoch Pratt Free Library, people said, "Oh, you're African American." But what was notable was that I was a woman. In a profession that started out viewing women as "genteel hostesses"—there's a feminist treatise on feminism and librarianship—women should feel welcome. Librarians rule.

Hayden, who ran the Enoch Pratt Free Library in Baltimore and served as deputy commissioner and chief librarian of the Chicago Public Library system, was the first African American to receive Library Journal's *Librarian of the Year Award in 1995.*

Mazie Hirono

First Asian-American woman to be elected to the U.S. Senate

"The Senate needs a lot more diversity, and I bring quadruple diversity."

I am the only immigrant serving in the U.S. Senate right now. I was almost 8 when my mother bravely brought her children to this country so we could have a chance at a better life. She figured out early on that she didn't have a traditional daughter. She never once asked me when I was going to get married or when I was going to have children. Not once. Why should she expect those things from me when her marriage was disastrous? She wanted me to live my own life, and she was supportive of every strange thing I did.

I got involved in the political arena in college, protesting the Vietnam War, and became friends with some of the activists at the University of Hawaii. We got together and said, "It is not enough for us to march and hold signs; we need to have seats at the table." Which meant that we wanted to prepare ourselves for public service. It was mainly the guys in the group who thought about running for office. I decided I needed more education. I went off to law school so that I could have more credentials.

Women feel we need to be much better prepared, that we need to have a lot of experience behind us before we run for office. When I first ran for office in 1980, there weren't that many women running for office. I had already run other people's campaigns, all men.

Having women and minorities makes for a fuller discussion, which leads to better decisionmaking. When I was first running for this Senate seat, in 2012, at one of the big gatherings, I said, "The Senate needs a lot more diversity, and I bring quadruple diversity to the Senate. One, I'm a woman. Two, I am Asian. I would be the first Asian woman to be elected to the U.S. Senate. Three, I am an immigrant. And four, I am the only Buddhist serving here." Somebody in the crowd yelled, "Yeah, but are you gay?" And I said, "Nobody's perfect."

There were five Democratic women running for open seats in our respective states. We would campaign together—Tammy Baldwin, Heidi Heitkamp, Elizabeth Warren and Shelley Berkley. The dynamic, the visual of all these women … It really hit people at our events that this is a powerful gathering of women who could work together.

Women are problem solvers. The women of the Senate get together on a regular basis. When the government shutdown happened, you probably saw the story of Susan Collins and others who worked hard to end that impasse. I think it's because women are not as ego-involved in terms of how to get things done. None of us is namby-pamby. We have different approaches, but I believe that women are very effective in what we do and in our ability to keep the lines of communication open.

There are seven women now on the Senate Armed Services Committee—more than ever in the history of that committee. It's a very macho committee. I believe that all of us women on the committee have experienced sexual harassment at some point in our lives, whether in college or wherever. And it's when the women sat on that committee that the issue of sexual assault in the military very much came to the forefront. It was really the women, in my view, who drove that issue, and got some changes made.

Clearly we have to make efforts to get women into the pipeline, whether in the corporate decisionmaking ladder or in politics. When you have a huge first like the first woman President, others will follow. Then there will be a second and a third and fourth. That is how things change, as far as the glass ceiling is concerned.

Hirono, who was born in Japan, was elected to Hawaii's house of representatives in 1980 and later became the state's lieutenant governor. She served in the U.S. House of Representatives from 2007 to 2013 and has been a Senator since 2013.

Mae Jemison

First woman of color in space

As a little girl, the idea that I might be the first woman of color to go to space would have seemed ridiculous. Of course we would have had all kinds of people up there by the time I was old enough to do anything! Growing up, I always assumed I would go to space. I wanted to do lots of things. Be a scientist, a dancer, a policymaker. I would make a difference in what happens in the world, and I knew that I could.

People might ask how I felt that way, since in the '60s one didn't frequently see images of women and people of color involved in science and technology. And yet I knew, because I had done a great job picking my parents. We talked about strong women. They made sure my siblings and I knew about the remarkable contributions that African Americans had made to this world.

Being first gives you a responsibility—you have a public platform, and you must choose how to use it. I use mine to help folks become more comfortable with the idea that science is integral to our world. And I vowed that I would talk about my work and ask other women about theirs—the nitty-gritty details. People say you can have everything. No, you can't. But you can have a lot more—and do a lot more—than you think.

Jemison, who holds degrees in engineering and medicine, went to space on the Endeavour *in 1992.*

Maya Lin

First woman to design a memorial on the National Mall

"I didn't try to look feminine.
I didn't want my gender to
become an issue."

As a defense mechanism when I was in my 20s, I would dress in an almost workmanlike way—Carhartt pants, work boots. I didn't try to look feminine. I didn't want my gender to become an issue. I compensated by dressing a little odd, a little messy. I still don't wear makeup, and I don't get dressed up for work. It's a bit of a uniform for me—my protective mechanism.

Architecture is a profession where you figure that whether you're a man or a woman shouldn't really matter. But when I was starting out, at the top firms, women architects were generally given the managerial positions, not the design positions. Why was it that women kept getting slotted not to be a design partner but a manager? You can still name on one hand the number of women architects who are out there as the lead of their firms. I was hyperaware of that from the get-go.

I'll never forget when I was an undergrad architecture major and we were going around interviewing construction managers and contractors … I was young and I looked even younger. A lot of firms, even the big ones, didn't quite know what to do with me. One firm decided to put out milk and cookies for me. For the first five, even 10 years of my career, I was almost always the only woman in the room.

When I won the competition to design the Vietnam Veterans Memorial, it was anonymous. You were a number. I was 1026. To this day I have to wonder, had my name been out there, would that have made any difference? Would my ethnicity have made a difference? Would my gender?

I was raised in a household where all that mattered was what you thought and what your ideas were. And you fought for those ideas. The memorial was built exactly as I had envisioned it, but it was a fight. Never, ever give up.

Lin won a public design competition for the Vietnam Veterans Memorial while she was an undergraduate student at Yale University.

At 21, Lin became the youngest person to design a memorial on the National Mall

Loretta Lynch

First black woman to become U.S. Attorney General

"It struck me most forcefully that the law must be for everyone."

One of the most significant moments for me was the first time I opened a trial on my own. I stood in court, in front of a jury, and said my name, and then I said, "and I represent the United States of America." It resonated within me to such a degree that I knew it would color whatever else I did going forward.

I was a very adventurous child. I am the only daughter and the middle child. I always wanted to do everything my older brother did. We're very close in age—he's only 18 months older—but I was always the one who got us into trouble. There was a brick wall right outside the carport at my parents' home in Greensboro. My favorite thing to do was climb to the top and jump off. I loved that flying sensation. I loved being able to see from up high. My parents had no idea, until one day I fell. I ran into the house to get a washcloth—thereby hastening my doom—just so that I could immediately climb to the top of the carport and jump off again. My mother was horrified. She put a stop to it for a while, but over time vigilance wanes. Pretty soon I was climbing that wall again.

My mother was an English teacher, and then a librarian. Our house was full of books. She taught me to read before I started school and that became my favorite thing to do—aside from jumping off the carport roof. I was one of those kids who asked for books for Christmas presents. For my mother, education was key.

One summer my mother went back to school to finish her master's degree in library science. She left us in the care of my father and spent that summer on campus so she could focus on her work. As a child, you're always stunned that your mother has any focus other than you. How is that even possible? But she did. And she did it in a way that never made us feel that we were not also part of that focus, and she made it very clear that one day we were going to be going away to school.

My mother was also a woman of principle. She followed my dad as he was a young preacher driving across the state of North Carolina, preaching revivals. She told me early on how, when she was a young wife and mother, she just decided she was done with the restrooms that were marked "Colored." They'd had to stop the car one night, and she went right into the restroom that was denoted for white women. The attendant, some young guy, was stunned, and said to her, "No, you're supposed to go over here." She said, "I don't feel like fighting flies," and just sailed on into the other restroom. She never used segregated facilities again.

My mother felt that if she was going to show her children that you can do anything, then she could not accept discrimination that has no basis in reality—no basis in anything. It had to start with her. She's always led by example.

My father was much more out front. He was a great influence because he supported me in everything I did. Even though I was the only girl, he never gave me the impression that I was limited in any way. The aspirations and dreams he had for my brothers were the same ones he had for me. The church can be a very traditional place, particularly for a Baptist minister in the South in the '60s and '70s. But I saw my father letting women preach from his pulpit. I saw my father advocate for women to serve in leadership positions in his church. For him, talent could not go unrewarded. So from him I got the view that there were no limitations just because I was a girl.

My father was always fighting a fight for someone. Maybe someone had been denied tenure, or there was a civil rights issue in our town. When I was a toddler, he opened up the basement of his church in Greensboro to the student protesters from North Carolina A&T State University who were planning sit-ins and marches and protests over the fight for desegregation. He thought I should see what was happening, so he would ride me on his shoulders when he went to those meetings. From him I learned that just because a cause seems difficult, if enough people are determined to do the right thing, you can change a great many things.

My dad told me that one of his earliest, most vivid memories was of my grandfather working with people who had gotten in trouble with the law. You're talking 1930s North Carolina—there were no Miranda rights in that day. You were at the mercy of whatever law enforcement stopped you on that dark road in the middle of the night. When people got in trouble, there was no due process, there was no assumed right to a fair trial or even a trial at all. It was a very, very different time. So people came to my grandfather for help. He'd hide them underneath the floorboards of the house where my father grew up.

The sheriff would come by—he knew my grandfather, because everyone knew my grandfather. His name was Augustus Claude Lynch. The sheriff would say, "Gus, have you seen so-and-so?" And my grandfather would say, "I haven't seen them lately." And the sheriff would leave.

As I got older, I would ask my dad, "Do you think the sheriff knew?" And he would say, "I think sometimes he did know, but he also knew that there really wasn't any justice in that area at that time."

A lot of people in the South were in that situation: when they were confronted with a problem, they had to leave their community, change their name, move farther north. It struck me most forcefully that the law must be for everyone. Obviously, we have to have accountability when something happens, but we have to have a system where you can have faith that you're going to be treated the same as anyone else.

In my father's community, people did not have that feeling, particularly people of color. That should not be the case. Not in America. That has stuck with me throughout my legal training and throughout my career.

Lynch served as U.S. Attorney General from 2015 to 2017.

"WHEN PEOPLE GOT IN TROUBLE, THERE WAS NO DUE PROCESS."

Rachel Maddow

First openly gay anchor to host a prime-time news program

"Being the first always creates a pressure that you don't want to be the last."

It's a credit to my employer, Phil Griffin, who hired me in the first place and is still the president of MSNBC, that he was willing to hire an openly gay host. There was no opportunity for them to hire me and have me be in the closet, because—I mean, look at me. I've been out of the closet since I was a teenager. They knew what they were getting when they took me on, and they've never made it an issue with me. I've always felt treated very well in the business along those lines.

That said, being the first always creates a pressure that you don't want to be the last. It creates a feeling of responsibility that you want to handle the trust that's been placed in you well, so it's not used as an excuse to keep other women or other gay people or other liberals out of the same business that you've broken into.

I never aimed at being in TV journalism, but I found myself here nevertheless. I feel I was very lucky to end up at this network, in large part because it afforded me the chance to work with and learn from Andrea Mitchell. She has done everything and been everywhere and pushed her way to the front of every line and elbowed past every other correspondent or security guard sometimes. I think she's a role model for anybody in this business, but particularly for women. I feel incredibly lucky to work anywhere near her.

Not enough has changed in the industry [since my career began]. There are definitely more out people involved in broadcast news and in cable news, which is great. But the number of women who are hosting, for example, prime-time cable-news shows, you can count them, because you're talking to her. That's it. So particularly when it comes to being the solo anchor of a news broadcast, the industry is still very male, and when women host cable-news shows they are very often paired with men, because they're not allowed to do it on their own for some reason. I think the industry is not static. But if you just take a snapshot right now of who's on TV, who's delivering the news, it looks like it's the 1950s.

A lot of what happens on cable news is, people debate about the news in pairs and in groups. I get the same sexist condescension that all women face in every environment. I don't think I get more of it than anybody else. But what happens on the air happens out in the open.

I think it matters in the TV-news industry not just that we get more women on television, more women anchoring their own shows, but that we get more female executives. There just aren't that many women at the top in decisionmaking roles. And when there are women in those jobs, they don't stay very long. That's both a symptom of what's going on with sexism in the industry and also the cause of why things don't get better.

In the political sphere, if you step back from individual races and look at the phenomenon as a whole as to whether or not American women are breaking through in political leadership, the numbers are not encouraging. I definitely think women are allowed to do a smaller range of things in public than men are and still be considered viable candidates. I'm struck by the fact that we haven't really made any progress in terms of women being as free to express an emotional range as men are and still be seen as politically viable. A woman's getting angry is seen as the end of a campaign, whereas a man's getting angry is either a sign of strength or a sign that he's been needled into losing his cool, but it's never been a sign of weakness.

I think we're kidding ourselves if we don't acknowledge that it's going to be an uphill battle for a woman, whoever she is, to win the presidency. I think there's a glass ceiling there that doesn't explain everything about the 2016 election—it's way more complex than that. But saying that gender isn't part of it I think is naive.

Maddow hosts the Emmy-winning Rachel Maddow Show *on MSNBC.*

Rita Moreno

First Latina to win an Emmy, a Grammy, an Oscar and a Tony

"I have a feeling that remarkable women very often have remarkable parents."

Nobody said I was going to be a star someday. Especially not in this country. I was just a Puerto Rican child. But I knew I was going to be very active in show business. I loved it. I was dancing for my grandpa from the time I was 4 or 5 years old in Puerto Rico.

My mother came to this country before I did. She left me with my father after she divorced him. My mother knew almost no English. She had no education whatsoever. But she had one skill. She could sew like a demon. She got a job in New York in a sweatshop. Within four or five months of coming to this country, she made some money, and she took the ship back (you did not fly in those days, who could afford it?) to Puerto Rico to bring me to the United States. She was a remarkable woman. I have a feeling that remarkable women very often have remarkable parents.

My mother was a delightful, enthusiastic, vivacious woman. She loved to laugh. She was filled with a kind of joy that you sometimes wondered where she got it, because she had such a hard time.

My mom helped me out in any way she could. She made all my clothing, all through my days at MGM. She made all my costumes. She was really good at it. She was unstoppable. And yet she was not a show-business mother. She was a very Latina woman who adored her daughter and did everything she could for me. She maybe did too much for me.

I was a very passive young woman, and I let everybody in the world tell me what to do. And I listened to the next person who said, "Well, you know what you really should do is …"

It did not serve me in good stead to say the very least. If I had had a manager, probably this person would have said to me, "O.K., you've played enough of those 'native' girls, now let's say no each time that's offered to you." But all I knew was that that was the only kind of employment I could get, so that's what I did. And

"I don't even mind saying that I'm envious."

so for years and years, I was really very miserable and hurt that I was only seen in one way and having to speak always, always with an accent. I couldn't even audition for anything that wasn't a "native" girl.

Managers in those days only handled big stars. You rarely heard of a young starlet who had a manager. So I had no advice from anybody. I had agents, and agents—if you're unlucky and I was one of the unlucky ones—are job-getters. They're not careermakers.

That's when you really feel helpless. You see a script, you see a small role for a young woman, you say, "Oh, I could play the heck out of that." And your agent says, "They don't want to see you." That's heartbreaking.

It also makes you very angry. So I was a very, very angry and resentful young woman for quite some time. And that's something that I had to really work on to try to, if not get rid of, at least temper in psychotherapy.

I pat myself on the back a lot for having been in eight years of therapy. It's very easy to just say, "I don't need this, I already have enough problems." But to face them and then to talk about them? It's very, very difficult to face your own terrible feelings about yourself.

I had no real role model. There was nobody that I could look up to and say that's somebody like me. There was no such person. Which is probably why I'm now known in my community as La Pionera, "the pioneer."

I really don't think of myself as a role model. But it turns out that I am to a lot of the Hispanic community. Not just in show business but in life. But that's what happens when you're the first, right?

I can tell you very sincerely that I'm envious of the new generation of Latina actresses because they didn't quite have to go through what I did. And I sometimes will actually say to myself, to be very honest, "It's not fair."

I have done nothing else in my life except perform. Which is unusual because almost everyone I know has been a secretary, an X-ray technician, something, anything in order to make a living. And I actually was able to make a living from almost the beginning, being paid for what I loved most to do.

I call myself the hardware shelf. There's a lot of awards and honors there. And I have earned that. I didn't ask for it, I didn't beg for it, I didn't pay for it. I earned that. People see the accomplishments—but it's good to remind people that so much strife and labor and tears and heartbreak came before that, that it really is earned. That's why I talk about this with ease. And I don't even mind saying that I'm envious, because I've earned that too.

I'm trying as hard as I can to keep pushing the boundaries of what a woman is capable of doing. And it turns out there's a lot we can do. There's a lot we can speak about. The way we're perceived is still in the ancient times, but I think we're on our way. We now feel so strong, and that we're entitled to feel as we do, whatever it happens to be. No one's going to tell me how to make my own choices. For too many years, everybody told me what to say and what to do and how to be.

Moreno is one of 12 people to have won an Emmy, a Grammy, an Oscar and a Tony, known as an EGOT. She received the Presidential Medal of Freedom in 2004.

In 1962, Moreno became the first Latina to win an Oscar, for her role in West Side Story

Jennifer Yuh Nelson

First woman to solo-direct a major Hollywood animated feature

I've been asked about the glass ceiling a lot, and I don't think of myself as some kind of crusader going around smashing glass. I don't feel like I had to—and that is a very, very strong flag showing the people around me made it so I didn't have to. Everyone I've worked with were the ones holding me up, saying, "Yeah, go!"

My producer for the first *Kung Fu Panda* movie, Melissa Cobb, is an amazing woman. She's supersmart and helps push everyone—male, female, anyone— to do their best. There was an animated opening sequence that had to be hand-drawn and outsourced. The directors were very busy, so Melissa said, "Jen, why don't you direct it as a sequence director?" I had a great time, the scene turned out fun, and people had a wonderful time seeing it. When the second movie came around and the director position was open, she said, "Jen, you should direct it."

And I'm like, "No, no. I'm too quiet, I'm too introverted." And she said, "You can do it. You have done it. That whole thing with the opening sequence was a test, and you passed." I thought, Oh, my gosh, you were testing me to see if I could do it! She said, "No, no. I knew you needed evidence before you could believe you could do it. I always knew that you could." That vixen! She's sneaky. When you talk about glass ceilings, she put me in a catapult and threw me at it.

Nelson's Kung Fu Panda 2 (2011) *is the second highest-grossing film directed by a woman, only recently surpassed by* Wonder Woman *(2017).*

Ilhan Omar

First Somali-American Muslim woman to become a legislator

"I said to my dad, 'This doesn't look like the America you promised.'"

L **ife in Somalia** before the civil war was beautiful. When the war happened, I was 8 years old and at that stage of understanding the world in a different way. We fled to Kenya and ended up living in a refugee camp for four years. We arrived in the U.S. when I was 12.

My family called me the "why kid" growing up. I always needed to know *why* something is happening, *why* I had to do something, *why* whatever. I still am that way. I constantly question myself, I question those around me, I question policy and reasoning behind everything.

I talk a lot about the men in my family because my mother died when I was little and my grandmother died when my aunts were little, so we didn't have those kinds of heads of household. But all the members of our household who were female were sort of living as equal, and as wise as the male figures in our family. We didn't really grow up in a gendered environment. We didn't have a hierarchy. My family is fearless. They truly believe that they have something to contribute to society and that it is an obligation as humans. I try to embed in my children that they have something to contribute. And that you give because you have to, not to be appreciated.

When we were going through the relocation process they do an orientation of what your new home country is going to look like. The America we were going to was very glossy and picturesque—the only things that existed were white picket fences and beautifully mowed lawns and everybody seemed to have everything that they need. When we arrived, our first experience was driving through Manhattan. There was graffiti everywhere. Trash everywhere. Panhandlers and people who were homeless sleeping on the streets. I remember looking to my dad for answers. I said, "This doesn't look like the America you promised." He said, "Well we haven't gotten to our America yet, you just need to be patient."

Somalia is a majority black Muslim country and so is the camp in Kenya. When you're growing up in an environment where your faith and your race are not topics of conversation, it's really hard to come to an environment where all of that means something. Being black in the U.S. means something. There's a history. Being an immigrant, a refugee, Muslim—all of those things represent an otherness that is not typical or easily confined into the social fabric of this country. As someone who grew up never really having to feel less than, it's a hard reality to wake up to when you're 12. I had to figure out what it meant to be a bridge builder—what it meant to forge relationships that really never existed becomes the backstory to how I ended up where I am.

People think of Minneapolis as a very liberal, progressive city. We have a lot of immigrants here. The incumbent I was running against was a trailblazer when it comes to women in politics, so you would think that my gender wouldn't be a big issue. But everybody wanted to make that an issue. To her, people were excited to vote for me because I was pretty. To the Muslim and Somali communities, my gender was a problem because politics is supposed to be a man's role. Then there was the typical stuff that women candidates deal with—as a mother, how irresponsible I must be to want to run and devote as much time out of the home. No one ever asks the male candidates who are also fathers how they expect to balance family life. Gender was a big thing.

People said I should be proud of myself if I got even 10% of the votes, but I'm pretty competitive. I wanted to keep going so I could prove them wrong. I ended up pushing all of the negative things aside because I kept thinking, regardless of whether we win or lose, this will shift the narrative about what is possible.

Omar was elected on Nov. 8, 2016, to represent Minneapolis' District 60B in the Minnesota house of representatives.

Danica Patrick

First woman to lead in the Indianapolis 500 and the Daytona 500

"You can't just be super-nice to everybody—not everyone likes you back."

When I was a kid, I tried everything: T-ball, volleyball, basketball, cheerleading, band, choir, track, tumbling. You name it, I did it. Racing was just one of them. My parents kept my sister and me very active, and it was a great way to be able to discover what I was good at. Let's face it—normally what we're good at is also what we love. People ask me all the time, "What's your favorite track?" and I go, "I don't know, whatever one I do good at."

I just got an email from a very old friend who actually helped me get my first major sponsor in America. He said, "You're just one of my favorites. I always liked talking to you and I'm always so happy for you. I was trying to get another girl into racing and she wasn't as dedicated as you were, she wasn't sacrificing what needed to be sacrificed. I'm sure she's doing fine, but she wasn't committed enough." I never felt like I was super-duper dedicated. I was just doing what I wanted to do. So it was easy.

I started racing Indy cars when I was 23 and I'm 35 now. When I first started, people asked about being a role model—"What do you have to tell young girls?" And I was like, "I'm a young girl! I don't know." I moved to England when I was 16, in my junior year of high school. I was out of the house, I didn't have my parents around. You learn in a crash-course style how to protect yourself, how to deal with the real world. It's not all kittens and rainbows. My parents say when I came home from England, I was cold. But I had learned that you can't just be super-nice to everybody—not everyone likes you back, or treats you well.

In the world of racing—having a sponsor and managers and people like that around me—I had to learn how to speak confidently. I can remember being told in the very beginning, "Don't go into a meeting and tell them, 'I think…' Say, 'I know…' You've got to be sure of yourself." That advice has always stuck with me.

In 2013, Patrick became the first woman to win the pole position at the Daytona 500.

Patrick, right, began her career racing go-karts when she was 10 years old

Nancy Pelosi

First woman to become Speaker of the U.S. House of Representatives

"When women succeed,
America succeeds."

When I was born, my father was in Congress. I learned as much from him as I learned from my mother because the two of them were very civic-minded—the value of public service, the idea that we have a responsibility to each other.

When I graduated from college, I got married and had five children in six years, so that was my life. I ran for Congress 30 years ago. At the time, my youngest was going to be a senior in high school and the others were in college. I went to Alexandra, my youngest daughter, and said, "Mommy has a chance to run for Congress. I would like it if it were when you were in college, but this is when the opportunity is. I love my life. Any answer is fine. But if it's O.K. with you, I'll take a chance and run." To which she said, "Mother, get a life." So I did.

People still asked, "Who's taking care of your children?" I'd answer, "My children are taking care of me." They always ask women that question: Who's taking care of your children? So I sympathize with young women who are running now who have young children. That's exactly who we want to be in Congress: women who reflect our population, young women with children who are in professions or who are choosing to stay home or whatever it is. Running for office as a woman is hard, because people trivialize everything that a woman has done. Not everyone places the value that I do on raising a family, which is a very major and challenging experience.

When I ran for leadership, some of my colleagues—even as enlightened as some of them are—would say things like, "Who said she could run?" As if I needed anybody's permission. And, "Maybe you could just make a list of things you want the men to do, and we'll do them for you."

There is a tendency to think that there's a secret sauce that only men know—that unless you wear a suit and tie, and unless you belong to the club, you really can't be serving the public. But that's their problem. Let them think that.

When I did break what I call the "marble ceiling," the response I got from the public was overwhelming, including the fathers who said, "Now I know my daughter has more opportunity." This may sound immodest, but in breaking that marble ceiling, we said that no longer does it always have to be—bless their hearts—white men in these roles.

When women succeed, America as a whole succeeds. It's an agenda that recognizes all the needs that women have. We need to have equal pay for equal work, and to raise the minimum wage so that women's work is valued. That helps men too. We need to have affordable, quality child care to truly unleash the power of women in the workforce. And we need to have paid sick leave so that if the breadwinner is sick, that person has the ability to stay home and not be docked pay or lose their job.

For women to be respected for the work they do, that is freeing. They can be entrepreneurial in their thinking. They can take risks. Our economy and society will benefit by unleashing the power of women. All the intellect, all the imagination, all the integrity, all the enthusiasm.

Nothing is more wholesome for the political and governmental process than the election and leadership of many more women.

So I say, "Be yourself. You may have role models and people that mentor you, and that's wonderful. But be yourself, because that's the most authentic person you can present. Value that. Know your power. And use it. America needs you."

Pelosi, who represents California's 12th Congressional District, has served in the U.S. House of Representatives since 1987. She was the Speaker from 2007 to 2011 and is now the minority leader.

Michelle Phan

First woman to build a $500 million company from a web series

I uploaded my first video in 2007. Social media wasn't even called social media yet. It was a place where people would just go online and congregate and share ideas and videos and content. YouTube was just my creative outlet. I didn't have sponsorship money, I didn't have people giving me free products. I had to go out and buy my own makeup products.

I was very motivated at a young age to find a better life, for my mom's sake. She wanted me to be a doctor, but I didn't see myself in that future. I promised her that I would take care of her but that I would still pursue what I loved.

Then I got this really amazing offer from a big beauty brand. When they told me how much money I was going to be making, it was so big—as much as a doctor would have made. The first person I wanted to tell was my mother. She's the reason I work so hard, and she inspires me so much. I said, "What are you doing?" She said, "Oh, I'm still at work, I'm doing someone's pedicure." I told her that it would be the last time she would ever have to do anyone's pedicure and she wouldn't have to work the next day because I would take care of her. We both started crying. It was a moment that I'll never forget. I want more people to have moments like that.

Phan launched the beauty subscription company Ipsy and the beauty brand EM Cosmetics.

Issa Rae

First black woman to create and star in a premium cable series

"I remember seeing a regular black love story and wanting to be a part of that."

I put up the first episode of *The Misadventures of Awkward Black Girl* on Feb. 3, 2011, and saw that it was surpassing the other two web series that I had done within the first day. It kept growing, and people were reaching out and saying, "This is me. This is my experience. I love this."

Hearing that positive feedback from black girls, black guys and then everyone else was an "aha" moment: they're relating to black people, at the end of the day. But I still get responses from people who think that because I have a show about two black women, I have to represent all black women. Obviously, we're not a monolith—we're not trying to be the end-all, be-all for black women's experiences in the United States.

I want to create characters that people can relate to. For so long, entertainment executives have said the reason they don't cast people of color is that they're not relatable onscreen. It's such a segregationist mentality, and I always knew that it was false. The first time I saw a movie that I felt related to me fully and sparked a feeling in me of wanting to create was *Love and Basketball.* I remember seeing a regular black love story and wanting to be a part of that, wanting to create that myself. I always credit '90s culture: *Martin, Living Single, The Fresh Prince of Bel-Air.* Seeing diverse representation of creators influenced me and made me feel like I could do this.

There's so much subtlety in the sexism and racism in this industry that you either have to call it out and risk being shunned, or move past it and find your own entryway. I'm definitely in the latter category. I put my blinders up and ignore it: "Nope! I'm going to do it anyway or find another way in."

Rae is the author of The Misadventures of Awkward Black Girl *and stars on HBO's* Insecure, *which she created.*

"I WANT TO CREATE CHARACTERS THAT PEOPLE CAN RELATE TO."

Shonda Rhimes

First woman to create three hit shows with more than 100 episodes each

"I wasn't trying to make
someone who was 'likable.'"

The set for the pilot of *Grey's Anatomy* was the big operating room with the gallery. On the first day, I think I must have spent about two hours playing with all of the tools, pretending I was a doctor, screaming, "Clear!" and "We've got to save them!" It was the best thing. You type in "OR day" and somebody builds an OR. You type "interior Oval Office day" and somebody builds an Oval Office. It's magical. You imagine something—and then it happens.

I didn't watch a lot of television before I started writing it, and I wanted to write people I wanted to watch. I was very surprised to discover that people thought Meredith Grey and Cristina Yang were revolutionary—they were like women I knew. Then I looked around the landscape of television and realized that a lot of the women were "nice." They were wives, they were people's girlfriends, and they were more interested in being mothers than they were in their jobs. That's fine—there are plenty of real-life women like that, but they just weren't women I knew. So it was interesting to discover that there was an issue about that.

The biggest moment for us was when we had one episode under our belt. My producing partner Betsy Beers and I were brought into a room at Disney—I like to say it was the Old White Men Room. Somebody said, "Nobody's going to want to watch these women. They're not nice, and nobody's going to want to watch a woman who sleeps with a man the night before her first day of work." I wasn't trying to make somebody who was "likable," so that was very strange to me. "Nice" had not occurred to me either.

As I sat there stunned, thinking, "I've got to get out of here," Betsy, to her wonderful credit and in much coarser language, said, "I slept with a guy the night before my first day at work." That's when I knew we were going to be best friends.

Rhimes created Grey's Anatomy, Private Practice *and* Scandal, *and is an executive producer of* How to Get Away With Murder.

Rhimes and Beers share two Emmy nominations for Outstanding Drama for Grey's Anatomy

Lori Robinson

First woman to lead a top-tier U.S. Combat Command

Family is my foundation. Early in my marriage, my husband was active-duty Air Force. We were stationed in Hawaii, and they were getting ready to move us—him to Korea and me to Japan. With kids, we just wouldn't be able to do it. I said to him, "David, I'll get out. I'm an air-battle manager, I'll be lucky if I'm a colonel. I'll never be a general. You're a Thunderbird pilot. You promoted early. You'll be the general." He goes, "And what would you do if you got out?" And I was like, "Well, I don't know." He goes, "Lori, I can go into the reserves, and I can go fly for the airlines." We never looked back. My husband was incredible. His constant love, devotion and support allowed me to move up in the ranks.

I've been privileged to be the first at many things. I'm a general, a commander, an airman. And I happen to be a woman. When I put the fact of being a woman as more important than the institution, then I've done a disservice to the institution. But I realize I'm a role model. I was in the Pentagon soon after I began working for the Secretary of the Air Force and the chief of staff of the Air Force, and people I didn't know said to me, "Congratulations. We've been cheering on the sidelines." All women. I had no idea. When I walk onto bases, a ton of folks come to me and say, "Ma'am, this is so awesome."

In 2016, Robinson became the highest-ranking woman in U.S. military history as leader of U.S. Northern Command and North American Aerospace Defense Command.

Sheryl Sandberg

First woman to become a social-media billionaire

"The world accepted that girls
didn't really do math contests."

I **was a nerd.** When I was in high school, I went to a math competition because my math teacher told me to. I liked it and I did fairly well, but there were no other girls. Even though my parents encouraged me to do anything, I came back and said to my math teacher, "Girls don't do this." He said, "You're right."

He was an amazing man and he really pushed me in math, but a better answer would have been, "And that's why you should do it!" But the world accepted that girls didn't really do math contests. We systematically treat girls and boys differently from birth—boys get paid more allowance as kids and do fewer chores, for example. Any woman in the workplace will recognize that pattern: we do more work and we get paid less.

We suffer from the tyranny of low expectations when it comes to women and equality. I remember in 2012, when women won 20% of the seats in the U.S. Senate. Fifty percent of the population, but 20% of the seats. All the headlines screamed, "Women take over the Senate, women take over the Senate!" Fifty percent of the population with 20% of the seats is not a takeover—it's a gap. Now, we should celebrate every Senate seat a woman takes, but the goal is equal representation. This is true in all industries. We should have half the leadership roles, and we're very far from that. But we will get there.

I came into the workforce in 1991. I looked beside me: equal men and women. The women were just as smart, sometimes smarter (no offense, gentlemen). I looked above me, and it was men. I figured, O.K., that's historical discrimination. My generation will change it. But as the years went on, there were fewer and fewer women in the meetings I was in. This stalling of progress for women in leadership led to my writing *Lean In.* Women had moved forward from the '60s or '70s till about 10 years ago, and they have stopped. We need to fix that, be alarmed by that, proclaim it as the really urgent crisis it is.

Sandberg is the chief operating officer of Facebook and was the first woman named to the company's board of directors. She founded the nonprofits Lean In and Option B.

Sandberg started her career at the World Bank after graduating from Harvard in 1991

Katharine Jefferts Schori

First woman to be elected presiding bishop of the Episcopal Church

"It was the lighting rod for conflict about leadership that didn't look like a straight white male."

I grew up in the Pacific Northwest, spending lots of time in the mountains and the islands in Puget Sound just fascinated with the wonders of creation. I was quite convinced that I wanted to be a scientist. Having a sense of the wonder of the world around us and the great diversity and the health that diversity signals translates into human communities as well. Being formed as a scientist prepared me in an unusual way to work in human community; being willing to have a hypothesis and test it and not assume that I know the answer going in has been very helpful.

The Bible says many things about women's roles. And the reality is, everybody cherry-picks. We all look for the pieces that affirm what we already believe. If we're faithful, we keep looking and hopefully we encounter things that confront us, that challenge us and that might transform our view of the role of every human being.

I read the narratives as saying that God has created human beings in God's image, that we are meant to be partners in caring for the whole of creation, that each person has particular gifts that may or may not be linked to gender, and that we're meant to exercise those gifts on behalf of the whole.

After I finished seminary, I received a call to go back to the congregation that I'd been a part of. And early on, a couple of older women came up to me and said, "We don't believe in women priests, but you're all right." It's the sense of seeing a real human being exercising a role you hadn't imagined women being in before that really converts hearts.

The day I was elected presiding bishop, after all the hullabaloo in the house of deputies when the consents were given, a man said to me, "Now, don't you wear dangly earrings." It just confronted his image of what was proper and appropriate.

I was elected in 2006, and Bishop Gene Robinson, who is openly gay, had been elected in 2003. That was an excuse around the communion for deciding that the Episcopal Church was heretical, that it had done something so offensive that it no longer belonged to the community, and the parts of the Episcopal Church that supported that decision didn't represent what other Episcopalians thought was appropriate.

So it was the lightning rod for conflict that was not just about gay and lesbian people but about leadership that didn't look like a straight white male, which had been the tradition for a very long time. I think it opened a lot of doors, and it's prompted a lot of creative conversation and some transformation.

Engendering opposition is a sign of being effective. If there's opposition, it means they're noticing that something has changed, that there's a difference. That's really the beginning of the conversation, if people are willing to engage.

I worked hard to expand the understanding of the average Episcopalian as to who we are as a body. We're not just a church in the United States. We're in 16 other countries. We come with many language traditions, many experiences of church and community, different cultural realities. I think we have a broader sense of the gift of diversity as a result, and a greater willingness to engage the different.

I know we're not finished, but I think maybe the piece we're wrestling with now is the full reality that every part of creation has a value and a purpose, and that we cannot simply treat other parts of creation as commodities as we have treated human beings in the past and still do in too many places.

I'm immensely hopeful about the coming generations of women in the church. They're bold and courageous, and they're willing to try new things and not take no for an answer. Those qualities are all very important.

Jefferts Schori studied biology at Stanford University and has a Ph.D. in oceanography from Oregon State University.

Cindy Sherman

First woman to break $1 million in a photography sale

"Of course we're all feminists, right? We all want women to be seen as equals."

I **never felt pigeonholed** as a child in terms of my potential. But I did feel that I'd probably be expected to settle down and get married and have kids at some point. I definitely remember from all the old movies and TV shows from the time, like *The Donna Reed Show* and *Leave It to Beaver,* all these women that were portrayed as these perfect moms. I never really saw myself as that. I never imagined myself getting married, I never imagined myself in a bridal gown, and I really never imagined myself having kids—and I never did.

In an issue of LIFE magazine, I saw Lynda Benglis as a young artist throwing paint on her floor. I don't know how old she was then. I was probably in high school, but it was the first time it dawned on me that a woman could be an artist.

When my career got started in the '70s, I did feel like I was being taken seriously. I didn't really notice any kind of difference between men and women artists until I would say the early '80s, when specific men started to become very successful. Even though I was critically successful, it was definitely a big distinction between what their work sold for and what my work sold for.

As I evolved in the '70s, I think I took for granted what the first wave of feminist artists had to go through. I never felt like an activist because I didn't experience that kind of fighting. It's not like I would say I'm not a feminist, I just couldn't quite identify with those women. Of course we're all feminists, right? We all want women to be seen as equals. I am shy and I'm not a person who can debate and take on critical political talk. But the same issues definitely piss me off and show up in my work, and I definitely have always used my work as a forum to address a lot of things that I can't say, that I can't articulate.

Sherman, who studied painting before turning to the camera, is known for her chameleon-like self-portraits.

"THE SAME ISSUES DEFINITELY PISS ME OFF AND SHOW UP IN MY WORK."

Kathryn Smith

First woman to become a full-time coach in the NFL

"My advice for women is the same as my advice for everybody: work hard, take every opportunity that comes."

I **grew up watching football,** going to college games when I was really young. It was something we did as a family. When I was in high school, I worked with my dad on the sidelines doing stats for high school games, and that really grew my love for that side of football—not playing but still being a part of it, the behind-the-scenes-type work.

I worked with the Buffalo Bills as an administrative assistant, so I knew many of them before my position changed and I became the special teams quality-control coach. They really embraced me as a coach, as another member of the staff, and not a lot of emphasis was put on the fact that I'm female and they're all males.

When I was initially approached about the special teams quality-control position, we did know that there hadn't been a full-time female coach. But it really wasn't something that we talked about. So it was a little bit of a surprise that it blew up as much as it did initially. We were not expecting that at all.

The Arizona Cardinals had Jen Welter with them in training camp in 2015 as an inside-linebackers coach. And there are so many females in the NFL. One of the Buffalo Bills owners is a woman, Kim Pegula. When the announcement of my position was made last year, Kim texted me, "Don't let it be about being a female. Do the best job you can. Show them through doing a great job that you deserve to be in this spot." Getting that support from her just really reinforced in me that I have the support of the team and the organization. Doing my job as best I could was going to be my focus.

It really hit me how significant it was when the attention was so nonstop. It was a story that hung around. I wouldn't say there's one moment, but over time it settled in that, wow, this was something that was pretty unique and pretty special.

I am aware that there have been some negative comments made from people who maybe didn't understand more and are questioning my qualifications, questioning my job. But overall it has been much more positive than negative.

Being in that position afforded me new opportunities. I interviewed with a young girl a few months ago for an Empower Girls program here in Buffalo. I was invited to go to the White House, which was a really amazing experience. But I'm glad that people are hearing my story—especially young girls, but even young boys and older girls—and can take something out of it as far as hard work and being able to fulfill your dreams is really special.

I've worked with a lot of women throughout my time in the NFL who I've seen grow in their positions and make great moves with different teams in the league. Just to see them excel and work hard and move on to the next level, that has been inspiring, and it shows that this industry is willing to reward people for their hard work—that the best person for the job is the person who will be hired.

My advice for women is the same as my advice for everybody: work hard, take every opportunity that comes. You don't know when something is going to turn into something else. You don't know when you're going to meet somebody who might be able to help you along the way. My hope for women in football is that we continue on this trajectory. As I mentioned, there are a lot of women in the NFL, and in professional sports across a lot of leagues. I hope it becomes less a story about being a woman and more of a story about doing a great job, about being elevated.

If you do the best that you can and you work as hard as possible, those opportunities will come to you. It may take a while. You will probably have to be patient. It's not going to happen overnight, but if you're persistent and you just keep grinding, good things will happen.

Smith, who began her NFL career as a game-day intern with the New York Jets, left the Buffalo Bills in January 2017.

Kathryn Sullivan

First American woman to walk in space

"The notion that women might menstruate in orbit drove the whole place up the wall."

In the early days, as one of the only women in a field camp or on a ship with all guys, I'd get a few reactions. Before, the men had permission to drop some social customs and be kind of locker-room-y, to use vulgar language if they wanted. One reaction was a "You're ruining my clubhouse" kind of thing. Another was "I don't know if we've got bathroom facilities for you." That was sort of astonishing. I thought, There's a tree right over there, and that toilet doesn't actually care who pulls the handle, and I think this will be fine. Places like a field camp, a research ship, a space shuttle—they are isolated environments for extended periods of time, and I think some men also worried about their wives' reactions to women now being there.

When we all joined the Astronaut Corps in 1978, NASA had the wisdom to bring in a critical mass—six women, three African Americans, an Asian. So there was a cohort, and we could build a bit of an alliance to tackle some of the issues that come along with adding new people to a close-knit culture.

I've heard stories about some of the preparations that NASA had to make to welcome women to the Astronaut Corps. There was an exercise facility that had only ever accommodated men and now was going to need some proportion of the locker room for women. It had a frosted-glass wall facing outward to the street. I don't think any woman had ever thought of going by there in the evening and gawking to see a silhouette of any of the guys, but as soon as it became apparent that there might be women behind this part of the locker room, there was a realization, like, "Oh, we need to do something about that, because guys might go gawk at women undressing." Well, wait—why was that not an issue when it was the guys dressing and undressing?

The really amusing stuff came, of course, in the onboard personal hygiene. You've packed a Dopp kit—they'd had a man's shaving kit for every spaceflight up until then. So NASA had a bunch of male engineers trained in the '50s and '60s asking themselves, "What's the female equivalent of a Dopp kit?" I would have loved to have been a fly on the wall as they tried to figure that out! "I don't know, what does your wife take on vacation?" The notion that women might menstruate in orbit drove the whole place up the wall.

There was a big debate about the dress code for women astronauts. A senior scientist at the Johnson Space Center named Carolyn Huntoon tended to be the go-to woman for advice in all of these moments. She said, "Well, what's the dress code for the men?" They said, "Oh, we never have a dress code for men astronauts." "Well, I think you have your answer."

"What if they wear something we don't like?" "Well, what do you do if one of the men wears something you don't like?"

"Oh, well, it's just not my business." "I think you have your answer."

"What do we do if one of these women that we select is married?" "You select her." "Well, what if her husband doesn't want to move to Houston?" "What do you do if one of the men's wives doesn't want to come?" She had to do that over and over, reminding them it's just symmetrical, people.

All six of us in that first batch of women felt a self-imposed pressure. One of us would be the first to fly, another would be the first to do a spacewalk—which only a small group of the Astronaut Corps gets to do. We knew our performance would have a big influence on the prospects of the women who would come after us. I was thrilled to be tapped for a spacewalk, but the "first female spacewalker" tag really didn't matter to me. It was my first spacewalk. And, sadly, my only spacewalk.

After 15 years at NASA, Sullivan became chief scientist at the National Oceanic and Atmospheric Administration and later administrator of the NOAA from 2014 to 2017.

Barbara Walters

First woman to co-anchor a network evening news program

The era of journalism I grew up in was dominated by men, but this did not scare me. The first time I felt like I truly "shattered the glass ceiling" was when I became the first female co-anchor of the *Today* show after climbing the ranks— I started at the show as a writer, and then reporter at large. I felt this same sense of accomplishment when I joined the ABC News family in 1976 and became the first woman in history to co-host the evening network news. I remember the exact moment when I signed my contract: I suddenly realized that my face, as the first female co-anchor, would be in millions of people's homes every night.

If I had told my young self that I would have the opportunity to interview every American President and First Lady since Richard Nixon, be able to do the first joint interview with Egypt's President Anwar Sadat and Israel's Prime Minister Menachem Begin, or my unforgettable sit-down with Cuban President Fidel Castro, I would not have believed it. Yet, I knew I was driven to interview world leaders and icons.

I am proud when young women journalists stop me and ask me for my advice. And I always tell them the same thing: go to work early, leave late when all your work is completed and do your homework.

After more than 50 years in journalism, Walters retired from her talk show, The View, *in 2014.*

Alice Waters

First woman to win the James Beard Award for Outstanding Chef

"I was very intimidated by cooking when we first started Chez Panisse."

I thought that when I graduated from college I would follow the path of my older sister: get married and have children. It was kind of expected that you would raise a family and then take care of the family and, probably like my mother, have a drink ready for my father when he came home from work. It never occurred to me that I would go down another path.

Then the Free Speech Movement happened in Berkeley, California, in the early 1960s, and I was on the edge of it. There was war in Vietnam, the civil rights movement and the general idea that the Establishment was doing things that were really immoral ... so I adopted a different set of values.

I was very intimidated by cooking when we first started Chez Panisse. We had Victoria Wise in the kitchen, and my partner Lindsey Shere was making pastries. I was in the dining room. We felt very comfortable in those places, in that place. But I was shocked when the French chefs came to the restaurant and said, "That's not cooking, that's shopping." I was aware that perhaps what we were doing was not complicated enough or not interesting enough. I have really come to appreciate that comment, however, because creating a beautiful meal is about finding the right ingredient, knowing when it's ripe and the exact way to use it. Nine-tenths of cooking is understanding farming and seasonality.

When I was invited to New York to receive an award, out of 25 chefs, I was the only woman. We each presented a dish. All of the men had fancy French dishes—ice carvings, sautéed lobster. I had brought a salad. I will never forget how self-conscious I was. I kept saying, "I borrowed the bowl from James Beard, I made the vinaigrette, and these are the kinds of lettuces." It was excruciating to think I had been so naive. And yet when they reviewed the dishes, all they talked about was the salad.

Waters opened Chez Panisse in 1971 and started the Edible Schoolyard Project in 1995.

Waters has infused her career with activism, advocating for sustainability and early education

Geisha Williams

First Latina CEO of a *Fortune* 500 company

"If someone else can
do it, why not you?"

I **was born in Cuba,** where my father was a political prisoner. When he was released, he and my mom decided that they wanted a better life for us. We came to the United States and ended up in Union City, N.J.

My parents worked very hard all the time. Somehow—and I'm very proud of them for this—they were able to save enough money to open their own grocery store. While other girls might have been heading off to Girl Scout meetings, I came home, had a snack and immediately went to work as a cashier in the grocery store every day after school. I joke with people that it was those early days at the cashier that made me really good with math because I had to make change on the spot. I learned at a very young age the value of being part of a community, the value of customer service, hard work and perseverance.

After I graduated from the University of Miami with a degree in engineering, I went to work for a local energy company. There, I had the good fortune of working for this person who ended up being a lifelong mentor of mine. He asked me one day, "Geisha, what are your long-term career aspirations?" And I said, "Oh, I don't know. Maybe I'd like to be a manager or a supervisor someday." He said, "No. I mean long-term."

Well, I was thinking long-term. At that time, women like me didn't run corporations. Latinas didn't run corporations. Immigrants didn't run corporations. But he looked at me and said, "Geisha, somebody has to run this company some day. Why not you?"

I couldn't believe that he had actually said that. But I remember going through the organizational chart of the company. I looked at their backgrounds, their degrees, their experiences. I noticed that a lot of them had engineering degrees. Well, I had an engineering degree. I thought to myself, Then why not me?

The industry is certainly very male-dominated. But I was comfortable in a male-dominated environment. I studied engineering back in the '80s, when there weren't that many women entering the STEM fields. I know that there were times when people felt that maybe I didn't belong there. And they might say something to make me feel uncomfortable. But I didn't let them bully me. I just took it in and decided to respond very professionally and respectfully. I just thought, I'm going to do what's right, I'm going to serve my customers, I'm going to work harder, and I'm going to overcome any adversity. I think I developed a certain level of confidence that I could do anything.

When I found out that the board had selected me to become CEO, it was such a "wow" moment. One of the very first people I called was that first mentor who told me I could do it.

I'm the first person in my family to go to college. I'm the first person in my family to be in any sort of position in corporate America. I'm the first in a lot of ways. I'm an immigrant who came to this country without being able to speak English and somehow—only in America, right?—I became the CEO of a *Fortune* 200 company.

You always hear people talking about what it means to be the first. But I think it's important that we focus on making sure there are others. While I may be the first, I certainly don't want to be the last. I would encourage young women to go for the tough jobs. The confidence you're going to develop as a result of doing a good job in those difficult positions is the confidence that you'll take with you to the next job and the one after that. It's like a muscle you develop where you start believing in yourself and your ability to do just about anything.

If someone else can do it, why not you?

Williams took over as CEO and president of PG&E Corp. on March 1, 2017.

Serena Williams

First tennis player to win 23 Grand Slam singles titles in the open era

"It isn't easy to be on the world stage and have people comment about your body."

I **am the youngest of five girls.** My sisters say I was a little bratty when I was growing up, but being the youngest, I always just wanted to be around them, always wanted to hang out. I started playing tennis because I always copied what they did, especially Venus. I wanted to be her twin. When she wanted to play tennis, I wanted to play tennis. When she played a tournament, I wanted to play a tournament. She's the only person on this planet who can relate to the things that I have gone through because we have gone through them together. I wouldn't be who I am today if I had to do it without her.

My dad put me in tennis when I was so young, so I always thought that was what I was going to do. There wasn't a moment where I decided to dedicate my life to it—I already had when I was 3 years old.

It isn't easy to be on the world stage and have people comment about your body. "It's too strong." "It's too much." There's always criticism about what I wear. Is it too sexy? Is it too fashionable? Is it too much? When criticism happens, I try to take a moment to appreciate myself. There will always be criticism—you have to have so much self-confidence and love for yourself. Once you have that wall of confidence, the criticism can hit against that wall and bounce right off.

I think the biggest criticism that I have received, along with my female peers, is when someone says that we don't deserve as much prize money as our male counterparts. In 2016, the CEO of Indian Wells said women players ride on the coattails of men, and thanked certain male players for carrying the sport. I have been in so many finals, either when I played my sister or other opponents, that were the most watched finals in the history of the tournament. So to hear that we as women should thank the men … I was like, Wait a minute!

I see these young women, including myself, who are working so hard and

"Growing up, I would have loved to have had a role model."

training for hours and hours every day just to have the opportunity to go out on the court and play their best. There shouldn't be any double standard.

My sister and I boycotted Indian Wells for 14 years due to a separate, unfortunate experience. But when I did return in 2015, I saw so many people—young kids, young black girls—so excited to see me. One girl was holding up a sign that said "Straight Outta Compton"—that's where my sister and I first learned how to play tennis. To see that little girl having the dream to play tennis too was incredible. In that moment, I realized my presence there was helping people. I was able to embrace that moment and fully appreciate it.

The world of tennis has come such a long way. We've had wonderful pioneers, such as Billie Jean King, who have been able to put us in the position to demand equal pay, equal prize money and equal big court appearances. We still have steps to take, but compared to other sports like soccer and golf, I think we've made some really big leaps because of our leadership. It is important for young black girls and young women of all races to have someone to look up to. Growing up, I would have loved to have had that type of role model.

Williams, who has been playing professional tennis since 1995, has won 72 singles titles, 23 doubles titles and four Olympic gold medals.

Oprah Winfrey

First woman in history to own and produce her own talk show

"I made every single choice of
my career based on my gut."

My significant personal "first" would be the very first time I actually hosted a talk show. From the time I was 19 until I was 24, I was a news anchorwoman. Everyone thought that being a news anchorwoman was the end-all be-all job. And even I thought that before I got the job, but it was very unsettling to me. I never felt comfortable in my own skin. It never felt authentic to me. I always felt like I had a pretend voice when I went on the air. I would interview people who'd been through tragedies or disasters, and I would feel terrible for them, and I would empathize, and then I would get written up by my bosses. So, I got demoted from the news job. They put me on a talk show called *People Are Talking,* in Baltimore. My very first interview was with the Carvel ice cream man and Benny, one of the characters from *All My Children.* It wouldn't have mattered who the guests were, because when I sat in the seat next to my co-interviewer, Richard Sher, and could ask questions just based upon what I wanted to know about ice cream and *All My Children,* it felt like coming home. When that first show ended, on Aug. 14, 1978, I said, "I have found my home. This is what I was meant to do."

I made every single choice of my career based on my gut. I would literally ask myself, "Does this feel right?" So when I got my show in Chicago, I built it around myself and the producers. We were young women in our 30s who were trying to figure it out and find our own way. We'd literally sit around and say, "What's going on in your life? What happened at the beauty shop this week? What's your mother talking about? What are your friends saying?"

It wasn't until the very first national *Oprah Winfrey Show* that I remember coming up with a sort of vision mission statement for what the show was, mainly because I was trying to explain to the national audience, who hadn't been watching along with Chicago for almost two years, who I was and what it was. I remember saying one of

"No matter where you are in your life — you are not alone."

the reasons I want to do this show was to let you know that you—no matter where you are in your life—you are not alone. Because it's the thing that I had discovered while doing the show. I learned so much about myself through other guests. I remember feeling for many years that I was the only person who'd ever been sexually abused. I didn't know that that was the language for it. But when I heard on my show someone else say the same words and describe the same thing that had happened to me, I felt, wow, I'm not the only one. And as time went on, over and over I would hear people share stories, feelings that I had experienced. The platform grew out of my desire to let people know you're not alone, there's nothing that has happened to you that hasn't happened to at least a thousand, perhaps a million other people, and the feeling is the same.

I remember going to my bosses once we were syndicated. Now, I didn't understand how much money I was going to make in syndication, because I'd been syndicated in Baltimore and nothing had happened with that. So the word *syndication* didn't mean that much to me, even though everybody was talking about how much money the show was going to make. But I started to see that that was really true. I was making a lot of money, and my producers were still getting the same salary.

I went to my then boss and said, "Everybody needs a raise." He said, "Why?" I said, "Because we're now a national show, and I'm making money." And he actually said to me, "They're only girls. They're a bunch of girls. What do they need more money for?"

This was in 1986. I remember going to my first boss in Baltimore in 1979 and saying that my co-anchor was making more money than I. This was on the show *People Are Talking*. I said, "Richard makes more money than I, and we're doing the same job. And so I feel that I should get a raise." And my boss said, "Why?" And I said, "Again, sir, we're sitting in chairs opposite each other, we're doing the same job. I ask as many questions as he does. Then I do the news, and he does the news."

And my boss said, "But he has children. He has three sons. Do you have kids?"

And I said, "No, I don't have kids." He said, "And he owns his own home. Do you own your own house?"

"I, uh, well, no. Well, I'm going to be buying a house."

"But do you own your own house?" he said. "And so, tell me again why you need more money?"

I said, "Thank you very much." And that is when I vowed that I was going to be leaving Baltimore. I realized, O.K., I'm not going to win. Who am I going to protest to? This is the general manager.

But that was such fuel for me. So when it happened again seven years later in Chicago, I go, "Well, either my producers are going to get raises or I'm going to sit down. I just won't work. I will not work unless they get paid more money."

And so they did. And while I was waiting for the bosses to pay them, I paid them myself in the interim.

A lot of things have changed since then. I think there are a lot of us of my generation and other generations who swallowed a lot. There's an old spiritual that says, "Trouble don't last always." I always knew there would come a time when I would be in a position where I wouldn't have to swallow it.

The Oprah Winfrey Show, *the highest-rated talk show in TV history, ran for 25 years.*

Winfrey's talk show was first broadcast nationally in 1986

Janet Yellen

First woman to chair the Federal Reserve

I had worked primarily as an economics professor and researcher before joining the Fed as a governor in 1994. This really marked the beginning of my career in public service, which was something I had always hoped to have the opportunity to do. It is a great honor to be part of the Fed and also a great responsibility to be working in the public's interest. Work at the Fed is not abstract; it matters to individuals and families and businesses across the country, whether it is through the setting of short-term interest rates, overseeing parts of the banking system or helping maintain financial stability. I have felt that same sense of awe and honor and responsibility every day since President Bill Clinton first nominated me in 1994.

I hope other women will have the same opportunities that I've had. I've been an economist for over 40 years. There has been considerable progress in increasing gender and ethnic diversity in the field. Unfortunately, women and minority economists are still underrepresented, particularly at the highest levels of academia, business and government. Many in the field are working together to understand and change that. I am encouraged by the American Economic Association's work in this area, and it is a priority for me at the Fed.

Yellen, formerly an economist at the University of California, Berkeley, is the chair of the Board of Governors of the Federal Reserve.

"IT IS SAFE
TO CLIMB.
COME ON UP,
THE VIEW IS
SPECTACULAR."
NANCY GIBBS